# GANDHI'S LEGACY

JOINT PASSIVE RESISTANCE COUNCIL OF NATAL & TRANSVAAL INDIAN CONGRESSES

# Certificate of Honour

## SOUTH AFRICAN
## PASSIVE RESISTANCE CAMPAIGN

COMMENCED 13TH JUNE 1946

# We salute and honour

........................................................

a brave fighter for freedom
who served ............... imprisonment
as a passive resister in
............... prison from ...............
to ............ for resisting the
racial colour-bar policy of
the Union Government and
particularly for defying the
Asiatic Land Tenure & Indian
Representation Act (Ghetto Act)

............................................
**CHAIRMAN**
NATAL COUNCIL

............................................
**CHAIRMAN**
TRANSVAAL COUNCIL

**DATE** ...................

# GANDHI'S LEGACY

## The Natal Indian Congress
## 1894–1994

Surendra Bhana

University of Natal Press
Pietermaritzburg

GANDHI'S LEGACY

ISBN  0 86980 931 8

Mr Nagin Devchand of Lenasia generously contributed towards the cost of producing this book, in the interests of promoting South African historiography.

*Cover photos*:   Local History Museum, Durban
*Cover design*:   Brett Armstrong

This book is printed on acid-free paper

Typeset in the University of Natal Press
Printed in South Africa by Kohler Carton and Print
P.O. Box 955, Pinetown 3600, South Africa

# CONTENTS

# ILLUSTRATIONS

Certificate of Honour,
  Passive Resistance Campaign                    *Frontispiece*

                                        *Between pages 70–71*

*Pioneer Presidents*
  Abdulla Hadji Adam
  Sarojini Naidu

*Early Stalwarts*
  Vincent Lawrence
  Albert Christopher

*Journeyers against Injustice*
  SAIC Deputation to India (1925)

*Division and Unity*
  NIA Deputation to J.C. Smuts (1943)

*Passing the Baton*
  A.I. Kajee
  Dr Y.M. Dadoo

*Leadership in Troubled Times*
  G.M. Naicker, G. Singh, M.D. Naidoo, A.I. Meer, M. Parekh,
  M.E.H. Ismail, N.T. Naicker, K. Moonsamy

*Defiance . . . and its Price*
  NIC Conference
  Monty Naicker leaving to face treason charges

*Links with the ANC and SACP*
  J.N. Singh
  Billy Nair
  Walter Sisulu
  A.J. Luthuli

*Onward to Freedom*
  Congress supports COP
  UDF rally

# ABBREVIATIONS

| | |
|---|---|
| ANC | African National Congress |
| APO | African Political Organisation |
| ASC | Anti-Segregration Council |
| BIA | British Indian Association |
| CBIA | Colonial Born Indian Association |
| CBSIA | Colonial Born and Settler Indian Association |
| CIA | Cape Indian Assembly |
| CIC | Cape Indian Congress |
| CPSA | Communist Party of South Africa |
| IEC | Indian Education Committee |
| NIA | Natal Indian Association |
| NIC | Natal Indian Congress |
| NIO | Natal Indian Organisation |
| PRC | Passive Resistance Council |
| SACP | South African Communist Party |
| SAIC | South African Indian Congress/Council |
| SAIO | South African Indian Organisation |
| TIC | Transvaal Indian Congress |
| TIO | Transvaal Indian Organisation |

In the dauntingly difficult task of reconstructing past events, the historian must place some reliance on the first-hand accounts of those who were involved. In making this study, I was indeed very fortunate to have the help of individuals whose assistance I gratefully acknowledge. They are: Ahmed I. Bhoola, Ela Gandhi, Pravin Gordhan, Ibrahim I. Ibrahim, Ahmed Kathrada, Hassen E. Mall, Ismail C. Meer, Billy Nair, Mewa Ramgobin, Professor Vishnu Padayachee, Cassim Saloojee, Hassim Seedat, and Dr Shahid Vawda. I am particularly grateful to Hassim Seedat, with whom I had many 'brainstorming' sessions about the project. Dr Farouk Meer was kind enough to arrange a meeting with some members of the NIC executive, although he was unable to attend.

I am very grateful to those who read the original draft of the manuscript and offered sound advice. Professors James D. Hunt of Shaw University and David M. Katzman of the University of Kansas made helpful suggestions, and Omar Badsha very kindly pointed out areas that required elaboration and improvement. Chapter three was revised and improved thanks to the critical reading it was given by Dr Uma Mesthrie. Pauline Podbrey very graciously offered additional information after reading chapters three and four. Hershini Bhana provided valuable insights into ethnicity and identity. Any shortcomings in the final draft are, of course, my own.

Professors Tom Karis and Gail Gerhart went out of their way to make available documentation for the 1980s, for which I am thankful. Dr Iain Edwards provided me with documents on the 'cabal' issue. Mewa Ramgobin also gave me some of the well-kept files which he had prepared for his defence in the 1985 treason trial in which he was accused number one. Chapter seven is the richer for their contents.

I am grateful to the personnel of the following documentation centres and libraries: the Documentation Centre at the University of Durban-Westville, the Department of Historical Papers at the University of the Witwatersrand, the Mayibuye

Centre at the University of the Western Cape, the manuscript section of the J.W. Jagger Library at the University of Cape Town, the Unisa Documentation Centre for Africa Studies in Pretoria; and the libraries of the University of Durban-Westville, University of Kansas, University of Natal, and the University of the Witwatersrand. I am particularly grateful to Dr C. Henning of the Documentation Centre of the University of Durban-Westville for providing photographs. Ms Gillian Berning of the Local History Museum in Durban went out of her way to assist me in getting some of the negatives processed.

I also wish to express my gratitude to the departments of History and African-American Studies at the University of Kansas which generously freed me of teaching responsibilities for a semester so that I could make a research trip to South Africa; and to the Hall Center for the Humanities for a grant which went a long way towards covering my travel expenses.

The manuscript was expertly typed by Lynn Porter of the College of Liberal Arts Word Processing Center. She and her colleagues, Pam LeRow and Paula Malone, rarely complained about demands on their time, and their positive and cheerful demeanour was always inspiring. Rita Chetty helped with the revision in South Africa. Dr Jenny Edley did a wonderful job of preparing the manuscript for publication.

Krish and Ramesh Bharatram, Savi and Alan Brimer were very supportive in my research endeavours. Professor Jairam Reddy kindly allowed me the use of facilities at the University of Durban-Westville. Naginbhai Devchand appreciated the historical value of the project and gave his generous support.

My research stay in South Africa made enormous demands on members of my extended family, and I express my deep gratitude to all of them, especially Neeru and Dips, Asha and Arvin, Bhanu and Jants, and Sumi and Sharmilla, Parbhoo-kaka and Masi. Dips and Arvin were particularly helpful in all manner of ways.

Finally, I was sustained and encouraged while I was away from home by the many letters of support received from Kala, Hershini, Hemant, and Palvih.

## CHAPTER 1

Introduction

# An Overview of the
# Natal Indian Congress

When the Natal Indian Congress (NIC) was established in 1894, it was intended to serve as a forum for the protection of rights the Indians believed they enjoyed as subjects of the British crown. Natal, like other parts of southern Africa, was, however, gravitating towards a white supremacist ethos. M. K. Gandhi had observed this trend, and had indeed been the victim of racial discrimination himself. He had completed the work that had brought him to South Africa in May 1893, and was about to return to India when he saw a notice of a bill before the Natal colonial legislature that sought to disfranchise the Indians.[1] He rallied leading Indian merchants to oppose the measure. They agreed, provided Gandhi would stay to co-ordinate and organise the opposition.

Gandhi and the Indian merchants met on 22 August 1894 at the spacious residence of one of the businessmen, Dada Abdulla. On that day, the NIC was born. Abdulla Haji Adam was its first president, and Gandhi was elected as its first honorary secretary. That was the beginning of an organisation which continued to exist for a hundred years through many vicissitudes.

In the early period, it was dominated by wealthy Indian merchants who hoped to secure the resolution of issues, largely in their own interests, by appealing to the imperial doctrine of equality. In the middle period from 1921 to 1961, the NIC experienced a gradual shift away from its reliance on the imperial connection to conduct a search for allies among the other black peoples. The organisation broadened its objectives to encompass a challenge to the racial system as a whole, and subscribed to the Freedom Charter of 1955. However, it was still involved with issues relating to Indians in its day-to-day operations. In the third period, 1971 to the present, the NIC emerged as one of a broad front of organisations working to destroy apartheid and to promote non-racial democracy.

The road the NIC has travelled has been long and difficult. There have been low and high points, marked by moments of acrimony and doubts, as well as by challenge and resolution. It has been a significant journey, and these pages hope to capture its essence. I have called this volume *Gandhi's Legacy* because throughout the history of the NIC, the influence of its illustrious founder has surfaced repeatedly. The South African Indian leaders periodically sought Gandhi's advice after 1914. In the 1920s, for example, Gandhi supported the idea of a round table conference; and, in the late 1930s, he dissuaded the militants from launching a passive resistance campaign.

Gandhi's influence in South Africa grew with his enhanced stature in India.[2] The NIC leadership has attempted to shape Gandhian ideas, and in turn has been shaped by them; and the discourse has been animated. But throughout the period, the leaders of the organisation have shared one Gandhian ideal: to resist injustice honourably and resolutely.

As background to the text of this work, some appreciation of the history of the arrival and settlement of Indians in South Africa is necessary. Broadly, two classes of immigrants came from India. The first was made up of indentured labourers who were brought to Natal to work on the sugar plantations. Natal joined the group of British colonies that were already making use of this form of labour supply. The first batch of Indians arrived in 1860, and, except for a short interruption between 1866 and 1873, indentured Indians continued to arrive until 1911. This pool of labour was drawn from districts in the southern part of India and from the Ganges valley. By 1911, a total of 152 184 Indians had arrived. The indentured Indians were used predominantly in the agricultural sector, but they were also employed in industry, and by the government. These migrant workers had the option of renewing their contracts, or returning to India. Those who chose to serve two five-year contracts were rewarded with a land allocation (an option open to them only until 1891) if they chose to stay in Natal, or with a paid passage to India if they elected to return. Many remained in Natal; others migrated to parts of South Africa beyond Natal in search of opportunities.

The second class was made up of individuals from western parts of India who paid their own passage fares and were therefore called 'passenger' Indians. They saw an opportunity to trade in Indian goods in the wake of the migration of their indentured compatriots. The passenger Indians began arriving in the 1870s. Many of the immigrants who were to run large trading enterprises were already established in Mauritius, or came via that island in the Indian Ocean. The largest numbers of the independent immigrants came in the 1890s. They did not have the capital resources of the earlier western Indian immigrants, and engaged in many forms of petty trade.

At the time that the NIC was established, there were over 42 000 Indians in Natal and an approximately equal number of whites. The struggle between these two immigrant groups took place in the midst of the vastly more numerous African population which now included the Zulu people, whose powerful kingdom had been systematically dismantled in the two decades after the British invaded Zululand in 1879. The whites in Natal, as indeed in the rest of South Africa, were in the process of consolidating their subjugation of the African people; and the appearance of the Asians simply complicated matters for them.

The white settlers recognised the value of indentured labour in Natal's economy. However, they were unhappy that so many elected to stay behind in the colony free to offer their labour in all sectors, or otherwise to engage in independent activity such as petty trade or market gardening. In 1893, there were 16 051 indentured Indians compared to 24 459 'free' Indians. Many of the passenger Indians had established themselves as traders. These 'Arab' traders as they were mistakenly called, linked up with white wholesale business to develop trade networks in the hinterland. Their customers were Africans, other Indians, and even whites.[3]

Since Asian immigration was an issue that went beyond Natal, the presence of Indians elsewhere in southern Africa needs a brief discussion. In the Transvaal, there were about 15 000 Indians, a great many of whom were concentrated on the Witwatersrand. Gold-mining had created opportunities for trade and work in the service sector; and in the Transvaal as in Natal, the Indian traders had also dispersed to small towns in rural areas. Their presence was resented, and the Boer government sought through Law 3 of 1885 to restrict the Indians to segregated areas. In the Cape Colony, there were probably no more than 5 000 Indians in the 1890s. Most of them were located in Cape Town and Kimberley. Many had gone to the diamond fields in the 1870s in search of work; and much smaller numbers of Indians had established themselves in trade as in Natal and the Transvaal. As for the Orange Free State, this Boer republic had barred Indians altogether in the 1870s, and there were only a handful in the 1890s. From Natal to the Cape, then, the white authorities increasingly positioned themselves in the 1890s to exclude Indians from their shores. Natal led the way, but after the South African War (1899– 1901) when all of South Africa had come under British control, the attempts became better co-ordinated.

It is important to recognise that, in addition to the obvious regional and class differences between the two categories of immigrants, there were also cultural, linguistic, and religious differences. Among the immigrants from the southern part of India were Tamil and Telegu speakers; and those who came from the northern and western parts spoke Bhojpuri and Gujarati respectively. They represented Hinduism, Islam and, in much smaller numbers, Christianity. India was overwhelmingly subject to the system of castes and subcastes; and the immigrants who came to South Africa brought with them this aspect of their cultural legacy. In short, the Indians in Natal were an extremely heterogeneous group; and this was soon to be reflected in the organisations that they created for themselves to fulfil basic needs of identity and sub-group cohesion. The NIC was a secular body that sought to rise above these cultural, religious, and linguistic differences; and when individuals joined this political organisation, or in any other way became identified with its aims and objectives, they did not leave their own associations, but added to their primary list of affiliations.

Given this enormous diversity, this study seeks to explore how and why the NIC was able to get the support of Indians who came to Natal. The diversity was marked at the beginning; and it did not diminish in the twentieth century. Rather, the Indians in Natal, and indeed in the rest of South Africa, assumed additional features to their identity which gave them commonality. Indians generally adapted to the norms and standards of the South African environment. In other words, they became 'South Africanised'. Whatever else this pejorative term may mean, it meant that Indians in South Africa acquired language skills in one or more of the indigenous tongues as well as English and Afrikaans. They knew and understood the political and social idioms that governed South Africa. Being persistently lumped together as an undifferentiated entity, the Indians increasingly saw themselves as one group of people who were obliged to respond accordingly. The NIC was to capitalise on both the assumed and imposed elements of this identity. Its politics revolved around it. For at least the first forty years of the twentieth century, the 'Indian' element of the NIC's identity was important; but its failure to make much headway in winning for the Indians the rights and privileges they were entitled to, stirred progressive Indians into seeking common cause with other disadvantaged groups and people. In the late 1940s and 1950s, the NIC entered into a multiracial alliance; and in the 1970s, the leadership of the NIC generally called Indians 'blacks' to show its solidarity with other black groups. This reflects, of course, the extent of the change of identity among South Africa's Indians. The dynamics of white politics, especially in the apartheid years, demanded such changes. But it would be a mistake to imagine that an altered political identity wiped away ethnicity. Many of the cultural and religious organisations that define Indians differently are still flourishing; and Radio Lotus draws heavily on the ethnic sentiments of a cultural legacy. In the wake of South Africa's first democratic elections, the debate as to whether the NIC has a place as a separate, ethnically defined organisation, continues. This study explores these and many other issues in its hundred-year history.

Chapter two discusses the early years between 1894 and 1914. In chapter three, the NIC's faith in the imperial connection is explored. The failure of that approach was to be the cause of much division in the 1930s. But out of the debate was to emerge new thinking among the NIC leadership. Chapter four looks at some of the people who articulated newer approaches; and chapter five examines the way in which they broadened the front to include the Passive Resistance Campaign, and the Congressional Alliance. What kind of routine business did the NIC undertake for its constituents? That question is the subject of chapter 6. The NIC experienced a resurgence after its revival in 1971; and it joined in with the Mass Democratic Movement of the 1980s. These developments are explored in chapter seven. Some concluding thoughts are offered in the last chapter, including what future may lie beyond 1994.

A word on sources is necessary. A study that focuses on an organisation should, under normal circumstances, rely on the body's own records in the form of minutes, memoranda, statements, reports, and addresses. The NIC's internal records do exist, but they are missing for much of the period, or when they do exist, they are silent on many details. This is not unusual in the life of a voluntary organisation. For the early period, I have relied on completed works, as well as established sources like the *Indian Opinion*, and the *Collected Works of Mahatma Gandhi*. These are unfortunately sketchy on organisational

*Introduction*

details. For the period from the 1930s to 1961, I have relied heavily upon the NIC Agenda Books. Annual conferences are well documented in fairly detailed minutes. They are generally weak on issues of finance and general membership. I did not have access to the minutes of NIC branches except those of Merebank, and those only cover about eleven meetings between 1955 and 1956.

Interviews with those who had personal experience provided some very useful insights and information, and I filled in as many gaps as I could by using such newspapers as the *Guardian*, *Advance*, *New Age*, *Leader*, and *Graphic* for selected years in the 1940s and 1950s. I paid particular attention to cultural markers in the newspaper sources. The *Indian Opinion*, *Indian Views*, and *Leader* (1974–84) carried commercial advertisements, and items of news reflecting Indian cultural, religious, and sporting activities. I concentrated on regular features, special stories, and the community calendar of activities that defined boundaries, ethnic or otherwise. I was particularly interested in how such boundaries resonated in NIC politics.

For the most recent period, after 1971, the minutes of the annual conferences in the 1970s are very brief and lacking in detail — perhaps deliberately so given the risks of state surveillance, an all too common phenomenon in apartheid's most repressive decades. For the 1980s, I had few official documents to work with. Fortunately, I have had access to information provided by some of the activists of the period. Their insights have improved this study immeasurably.

## CHAPTER 2

# The Search for Imperial Brotherhood

## 1894 to 1914

What we wanted in South Africa was not a White man's country; not a White brotherhood, but an Imperial brotherhood.

Gandhi, October 1901

. . . this country is the Kaffirs'. We Whites are a handful. We do not want Asia to come in.

Smuts to Gandhi, 19 April 1911

Abdulla (often spelled Abdoola in early records) Hajee Adam, the first president, was assisted by twenty-three vice-presidents, an honorary secretary, and thirty-seven other members of the 'Congress Committee'. A body of fifty-two was obviously much too large to carry out the day-to-day operations of the NIC.[1] The work was probably entrusted to a small core of the Congress hierarchy. In practice, one suspects that most of the duties were performed by M.K. Gandhi, the NIC's energetic secretary, whose work was thorough and meticulous. Besides, he had undertaken to serve the community in this fashion without remuneration in the expectation of being retained for his legal work by the Indian merchants.[2] The committee was expected to meet at least once a month; and the general membership was to be kept minimally informed about the organisation's affairs at one annual general meeting.

One of the main purposes of the NIC was to ensure a better understanding of the position of the Indians by Natal's white colonists. At the time the NIC was founded, some whites tended to perceive it as a secret organisation with sinister motives. But the organisers sought to reassure them that their purpose was indeed to promote 'concord and harmony' with whites, and toward this end they were prepared to invite one of them to serve as a vice-president. I am not sure whether an invitation was actually extended, but no white person appears to have served on the NIC executive.[3] The organisers listed among the objectives of the NIC, a desire to maintain the Indian heritage. The expressed intention to establish a library was in part to fulfil this obligation. While it was important for Natal's Indians to know about India, it was also essential to keep India informed about developments in the British colony. Beyond these objectives there were others; among them vigilance over the living conditions of Natal's Indians generally, and of the indentured and the 'poor and helpless' specifically.[4]

The NIC's official aim was to reach all Indians, but the organisation's high subscription rate undermined that ambition. The membership fee was five shillings per month or £3 per year, an amount that was beyond the reach of most Indians, whose average income in the 1890s was around £10 per annum. Some time later, the organisation considered accepting small donations of one and two shillings to involve 'Tamil members', but this gesture probably did not result in the extension of membership to them. In reality, it was the leading merchants who made up the financial backbone of the NIC, and the net was cast widely to incorporate those in Verulam, Pietermaritzburg, Newcastle, and Charlestown. The organisers expected to have regional branches, and perhaps there were a few, although the official NIC reports are silent about them. In practice, the NIC was Durban-centred with most decisions originating among the executive members located in the city.[5]

Since membership was connected to revenue-gathering, the organisers were not above cajoling individuals into joining during the early years. At Tongaat, Kasim Bhan's store was 'occupied' overnight and until noon the next day when he relented and joined the NIC.[6] There were 228 members in 1895, who were responsible for paying nearly £536 in membership dues. Another amount of nearly £87 came in as donations, but it seems that the total of over £616 was not enough to cover the expenses of all the activities that Gandhi had in mind. He believed that the NIC needed something like £4 000, and suggested that the merchants should donate five shillings to the organisation for every £100's worth of goods they sold.[7]

By September 1901, the NIC could record 723 'subscribers' and a cash balance of £3 404.[8] The organisation had bought property to the value of £1 080, and collected £10 in monthly rental from its mainly Tamil tenants. The NIC moved into more spacious quarters at a £5 monthly rental, and subsequently held meetings at 'Congress Hall'.[9] In spite of these revenue-earning investments, the NIC was in debt for much of the first decade of the twentieth century, and its membership dwindled. This had much to do with the NIC's conservative orientation, and its apparent desire to maintain a restrictive membership policy.

Naturally, there were instances when the NIC's restrictiveness was debated, especially among those who felt left out. One such occasion was in 1907 when a group of Indians, represented by V. Lawrence, wrote a letter to the *Natal Advertiser* expressing dissatisfaction over the non-representation of 'colonial Hindus and Christian Indians' in the NIC. Lawrence revealed that he and two others, B. Gabriel and A.D. Pillay, had met with the NIC to discuss how it could be made more representative. At an NIC meeting held subsequently on 8 April 1907, a resolution was passed to admit young individuals at reduced subscriptions, and was referred to a committee of eight. Nothing more is heard about the issue, but the establishment of the Natal Indian Patriotic Union in 1908 suggests that the NIC was unable to resolve the issue to the satisfaction of those who felt shut out.[10] In a loosely related issue, a group calling itself Main Line Indians, in Natal's interior along the railway route to the Transvaal, wanted in

1909 greater representation on the committee, but its concern appears to have been connected with its desire to have a greater say in executive decision-making, especially in money matters.[11]

Given the high subscription rates and the restrictive membership, what kind of backgrounds did those in the NIC leadership have? A brief examination of those who held the presidency suggests that the NIC wanted to maintain an image of itself as an organisation made up of solid, successful, and reasonable individuals. All the presidents were part of the well-to-do commercial élite with business interests in Natal and other parts of southern Africa. Many of these were already prominent in the Durban Indian Committee, the merchant-run organisation that preceded the NIC by three years.

The first president, Abdulla Haji Adam was one of two managers in the firm of Dada Abdullah and Company, which had fifteen branches scattered throughout Natal, and also managed two steamers that operated between Durban and Bombay. He was followed by his brother, Abdul Karim Hajee Adam for a brief period. The third president was Cassim Mahomed Jeewa who held the office until 1899. Abdul Kadir (sometimes spelled Cadir) next held the presidency until 1906, and was followed by Dawad Mahomed who was the president until 1913. Not much is known about Jeewa; but Kadir and Dawad Mahomed were prosperous businessmen. Kadir was a partner in the firm M.C. Camroodeen and Company, which held interests in the Transvaal as well. Dawad Mahomed was a partner in the firm Ismail Mamoojee and Company in Pretoria, and later established his own business in Natal. An analysis by Maureen Swan of the average annual income of 1 800 of the commercial élite shows that it was over £300 in contrast to the average Indian income of £12 to £18 per annum.[12]

Of those who held the secretary's position, many also had business backgrounds with the added qualification of being fluent in English. Adamji Mian Khan (1896–97) was a partner in G.H. Miankhan and company. O.H.A. Jhavery (1906–1907) worked with Dada Abdullah's firm, and made two trips to India to improve his educational qualifications. In the early 1900s, he ran the 'Kaffir' market in Queen Street, Durban. Mahomed Cassim Anglia (1909–1914), who was fluent in English, Dutch, French, and several Indian languages, was a managing partner of a Mauritian sugar merchant, and later ran a business in Durban. Dada Osman, who replaced Jhavery as secretary in 1907, spent a few years with Dada Abdullah and Company before he established a business of his own. He operated two branches in 1898, one in Umsinga and another in Vryheid. The three individuals who did not have commercial businesses of their own were Gandhi, M.H. Nazar (1901–1906), and R.K. Khan (1901–1905/6). Nazar, who was fluent in English, became the first editor of *Indian Opinion*; and Khan was an attorney who came to Natal with Gandhi's help.[13]

With the substantial representation and even over-representation of the commercial élite on the NIC executive, it is not surprising that the NIC was concerned with the issues that most affected their interests, namely trade and immigration. Towards the resolution of these issues, it spent money submitting petitions and memorials to colonial and imperial officials, lobbying prominent individuals and government officials through paid agents, and sponsoring deputations in 1906 and 1909. In Gandhi, the NIC found a competent propagandist for the organisation, who went to India on two separate occasions, and made two trips to London. On Gandhi's first return visit to India, for example, the NIC secretary produced *The Grievances of the British Indians in South Africa: An Appeal to the Indian Public*, (popularly referred to as the Green Pamphlet), for the publication of which the organisation paid £1 766.[14]

All of this gave the NIC a high profile, not only in South Africa, but in England and India as well. Influential individuals came to view the NIC as being representative of all South Africa's Indians. Alternative organisations established by dissident groups in the early years of the twentieth century received little attention abroad and consequently did not enjoy much success. The NIC declared an interest in the welfare of indentured Indians, who had no political organisation of their own, yet did little more than express concern about their ill-treatment. Later it advocated termination of their immigration to improve its own political leverage, and only belatedly supported the abolition of the £3 tax that affected them. So, while the NIC remained a visible organisation overseas, by 1910 it did not enjoy the support of the majority of South African Indians. The crisis in the organisation came towards the end of 1913, when the satyagraha campaign expanded to embrace issues and strategies with which the commercial élite could not identify.

The white colonists in Natal had begun to express fears in the 1890s about being swamped by Indian immigrants. The artisans among them feared losing their jobs to free Indians, or other Indians specially imported to do skilled or unskilled work over which they believed they should have some kind of monopoly; and the traders among them felt threatened by 'Arab' merchants whose capital and resourcefulness could capture the trade with Africans. After responsible government was introduced in 1893, these elements in Natal's white population exercised greater influence in the legislative decision-making. They increasingly pressed the colonial authorities to adopt measures that addressed their concerns, and prevailed upon Whitehall to endorse them. Four measures were adopted before 1899 by the Natal legislature, and these came to dominate much of NIC politics before and after that date. The four laws were: The Franchise Law Amendment Act of 1896, Act 17 of 1895, the Immigration Restriction Act (Act 1) of 1897, and the Dealers' Licences Act (Act 18) of 1897.[15]

The bill to disfranchise the Indians was first introduced in the Natal legislature in 1894, but was disallowed because it made direct reference to Indians which in theory was contrary to the principle of Imperial equality. Natal, however, used a device that did not refer specifically to Indians but which nevertheless had the effect of excluding them from the franchise, namely, of disqualifying those whose native countries had not 'hitherto possessed elective representative institutions'. In Durban, at the time, only 251 Indians were registered as voters, and in the capital, Pietermaritzburg, only 31 in contrast to 7 000 and 300 white voters respectively in the two cities. But as small as their numbers were, the Indian voters were perceived as a future danger.[16]

The Natal whites did not object to the presence of the indentured Indians, whose value to the colony's economy was openly acknowledged. But they did not approve of the option to settle in Natal given to the ex-indentured. Since the government of India would not agree to compulsory repatriation, the Natal government passed Act 17 of 1895, which required indenture-expired Indians to pay a tax of £3. (The original amount was £25, but the government of India opposed it.) The law was to come into operation in 1901, after which those who terminated their contracts were required to pay the tax, or return to India if they did not wish to re-indenture.

The other two laws were aimed at passenger Indians without, of course, specifically referring to them. The Immigration Restriction Act of 1897 empowered the immigration officer to apply a simple literacy test at the point of entry. The fact that no Indian language was to be used made it clear that the law was meant to exclude the independent Indian immigrants, who, it was believed, merely swelled the numbers of the 'Arab' merchants. Colonial Secretary Joseph Chamberlain approved of the 'Natal formula', and recommended it to other British colonies similarly interested in restricting Asian immigration. While the immigration law was designed to exclude potential Indian traders, the Dealers' Licences Act of 1897 was enacted to curtail the growth of 'Arab' trade. The law empowered a licensing officer to review licences annually and gave him the authority to refuse renewals on any number of grounds from personal hygiene to the nature of the trade. The applicant had no recourse to judicial review in the event of refusal, and the licensing officer was not obliged to furnish any reason for refusal.[17]

These Natal laws raised issues of political disability, immigration and trade restrictions, and an unfair tax which carried with it a penalty for choosing to settle in the colony. If one adds to these a few more like the threat of establishing segregated locations (the ghost of the Transvaal Law 3 of 1885), the prohibition of inter-state travel, and the absence of basic facilities in education, health and housing, one sees the whole range of major issues that confronted the Indians in this early period, and around which much of the politics is centred. The growing segregationist tendencies imposed a variety of disabilities, and there were frequent complaints about them in letters to the press, or memorials to the authorities. Their political powerlessness rankled among the Indians, and they realised that many of their disabilities flowed from it, but no political organisation, certainly not the NIC or the BIA, ever took it up as a serious issue. Indeed, the leaders in the two organisations frequently reassured the white authorities that it was not their intention to challenge the latter's political domination.

How did Indian leaders and organisations, especially the NIC, respond to the disabilities referred to above? The response can be broadly divided into two categories: firstly, the overall philosophy that informed the legal-constitutional approach that is apparent throughout the period but most especially in the early years; secondly, the direct challenge to authority as evidenced in the satyagraha campaign, 1906/7–1914. While, of course, concentrating on the NIC, the discussion must perforce range beyond Natal. After 1907, the political movement spread beyond Natal, and the NIC responded to this development.

Before discussing the two broad categories, a slight digression must be made with reference to Gandhi. He played an influential role in shaping the NIC strategy until 1899; and even though he resigned his secretaryship and moved to the Transvaal in 1903, soon after his second return from India, he nevertheless continued to make a contribution to NIC policies at least until 1910. In the Transvaal, he helped in the foundation of the British Indian Association (BIA) in 1903, and became its secretary. It dawned on him that the struggle was larger in scope than originally envisaged and involved the whole of South Africa. With this in mind, he attempted to co-ordinate the campaign. In the Transvaal he had influence over the BIA; in Natal he worked through the NIC among other organisations; and in the Cape, through organisations like the British India League. He made frequent visits to Natal where, after June 1904, he also managed the *Indian Opinion*, and supervised the experiment in communal living at Phoenix near Inanda. He rarely failed to meet with the NIC leadership whenever he was in Natal, or to address meetings held under the organisation's auspices. Above all, he held considerable sway over its leadership, if not the rank and file, through the columns of the *Indian Opinion* in which he maintained a ceaseless barrage of comments on and interpretations of events in South Africa.

While Gandhi's role was influential, it was not central in the sense that the movement for the entire period was not controlled by him. There has been a tendency in early works on Gandhi to see the movement in monolithic terms, and his role as pivotal. I am largely in agreement with Maureen Swan whose seminal work has shown the existence of an intricate network of political, semi-political, religious, and ethnic organisations whose perspectives Gandhi could not ignore.[18] However, Swan's work focused on group formation around materialist interests, and tended to minimise the role of organisations primarily driven by cultural and religious considerations. This study will show that these were central to South African Indian politics. Gandhi understood well the diversity among Indians and, in his drive to unite them, he worked with rather than against it. Indeed, he had to move from one group to another as he sought to maintain alliances and support. He had to adjust to altering circumstances; and his ability to do so was a reflection of his greatness.

Furthermore, there were other voices, and other bodies beyond the NIC. P.S. Aiyar, for example, ran the *Colonial*

*Indian News* from 1901 to 1903, and was not a man who could be ignored. In 1907, he established the *African Chronicle* the columns of which he used to reflect on issues on which he differed from the NIC and Gandhi. He was a founding member of three separate organisations, all of which challenged the NIC. These were: the Natal Indian Patriotic Union (NIPU, f.March 1908), Colonial Born Indian Association (CBIA, f.March 1911), and South African Indian Committee (SAIC, f.October 1911). V. Lawrence, Lazarus Gabriel, and R.N. Modaley, were some of the other voices, and they too were founding members of at least two of the above organisations.[19]

While there were many who disagreed with him, there were others who were drawn to him. Gandhi was an extraordinarily energetic individual, who used his singlemindedness of purpose with persistence. He constantly thought up innovative ways of tackling problems. Of course, he had his low periods when he withdrew within himself. One such occasion was when the satyagraha campaign had virtually collapsed by 1910. He spent long spells of time at the Tolstoy Farm near Lawley, Johannesburg, in experimental communal living. But the source of his strength was his spirituality, and increasingly he wrote and reflected on religious matters in the *Indian Opinion*. Gandhi's moral philosophy grew in depth and conviction. His political views matured, showing remarkable growth between 1904 and 1910. The point to be emphasised is that the force of his extraordinary personality cannot be ignored because of the way in which it made an impact on his supporters. Something of that is apparent in the reverence that thousands of indentured Indians showed for him in 1913 and 1914. Swan recognised this but shifted the focus to Gandhi's status rather than his personality.

## Legal-Constitutional Approach: Looking Abroad
Throughout the period under discussion, the laws and practices that singled out Indians for differential treatment were opposed on the grounds that Indians as British subjects

enjoyed protection under the doctrine of Imperial equality, and that Whitehall should uphold this principle in colonies under its control. The rights and privileges enjoyed by Indians as British subjects in India did not cease to exist when they moved to another part of the empire. Laws in the colonies that violated this principle were unconstitutional, and un-British. Beyond this legal point, the importance of maintaining Imperial unity was stressed. India was important to the empire, and the Imperial government should guard against things that might offend its Indian subjects.

This was, of course, Gandhi's position. He admired the British empire, and implicitly accepted the benefit of an Imperial brotherhood that transcended race and ethnicity. That was the spirit in which he, with the support of the NIC, organised an ambulance corps in 1899 when the British fought against the Boers, and again when Natal crushed the 'Bambatha' rebellion in 1906. In 1911, when King George V was crowned, the NIC did not object to celebrating the event, but opposed the segregated ceremony organised by the Natal authorities. Indians wanted to show their loyalty to the British crown.[20]

The NIC, as well as the BIA, supported this approach. They petitioned the British government not to allow laws that discriminated against British Indian subjects. Between 1900 and 1910 especially, they pleaded for protection against a developing racial system in South Africa. The NIC and the BIA lobbied influential individuals in Britain and India. Deputations were sent in 1906 and 1909 to London. Gandhi was particularly interested in mobilising the Indian National Congress to lobby the Viceroy to take up the South African Indian case. He did not have much success with nationalist leader Pherozeshah Mehta, but was successful with Gopal K. Gokhale, who not only became his political mentor, but was prepared, as a member of the Imperial Legislative Council, to take up the Indians' cause with the South African government when he visited in 1912. The South African British Indian Committee (SABIC) was created in London to lobby for the

Indians. The NIC contributed funds towards the maintenance of the SABIC. In 1909/10, the NIC requested H.S.L. Polak, who was then in India, to represent its interests. And the NIC officials regularly met with colonial officials in Natal.

If this approach was not entirely successful, it was because the emergent South African politics were involved in a dynamic that did not hold out much hope for the Indian cause. The British had managed to impose hegemony over South Africa after a costly war with the two Boer republics. After the war, Britain realised that its continued influence in the region depended on Boer-Briton amity, and neither the Boers nor the English-speaking whites were willing to yield on the Indian question. And Britain was not likely to jeopardise its interests by championing the Indians in South Africa.

The narrow base of the NIC is reflected in the issues it took up most strongly. Dominated as it was by merchant interests, immigration and trade received most attention, especially the latter. Trade restrictions imposed on prominent businessmen were highlighted. The *Indian Opinion* gave publicity, for example, to the Somnath Maharaj and the Hoondamal cases. Maharaj was prevented in 1898 from trading on premises owned by the NIC on the grounds that there was already sufficient trade in the area; and Hoondamal was stopped from moving his business from Grey Street to West Street in 1904/5. Wherever possible, legal recourse was taken. The campaign succeeded in the end because the Natal legislature was forced by the British government to allow licence appeals to be heard in the law courts, and thus checked some of the arbitrariness with which licences had been refused in the past. In a related case, the BIA tested the legality of the administration's provision to confine Indian businesses to locations. The Transvaal Supreme Court decided in favour of Habib Motan in 1904. Motan was free to trade outside of segregated locations.

The NIC showed some paternalistic concern for the indentured Indians. It occasionally took up individual cases of physical abuse against them with the Protector of Indian Immigrants. It expressed concern about the high rate of suicide among the contract workers, and called for an official inquiry. The NIC did, however, take a strong stand against the continued importation of indentured workers. This move was motivated in part, if not in its entirety, by the NIC's desire to exercise some leverage on the Natal legislature over the licence issues. As for the £3 tax, which seriously affected indentured Indians, the NIC supported its abolition especially after 1910. But since a separate Anti-£3 League was established in September 1911, it is not clear how strongly it was committed to its stand.[21] Many of the NIC's commercial élite were keenly aware of the social distance between them and the indentured Indians, and probably did not think seriously of them as potential political allies. Gandhi's call on the indentured Indians to join the campaign late in 1913 alarmed these members of the NIC as they believed that the consequences of the action would hurt their interests.

On another issue, namely the failure to search for allies from among other blacks, there was unanimity among all Indian leaders and organisations. All of them adopted the strategy of looking abroad for help. The Imperial forum was the right place, they believed, in which to air their grievances and India's importance in the empire could be an effective lever. Gandhi's thinking on this issue was certainly representative of the Indian leadership. Gandhi knew about the African Political Organisation (APO), and had great respect for its leader, Dr Abdulla Abdurahman; but the 'coloureds' were 'children of the soil' he said, and what was appropriate for them was not suitable for the Indians. The coloureds should not be 'lumped' with the Indians, he insisted, because 'they have different points of attack in their struggle for freedom of existence'.[22]

What did the Indians think of the other 'children of soil', namely the Africans? Again using Gandhi as an exemplar of Indian thinking, there is no evidence to show that the possibility of Africans as potential allies was even considered. Gandhi referred to Tengo Jabavu in relation to his efforts to establish an inter-state college for Africans, but beyond that there is no reference to African political organisations, or to African political aspirations. He was surely aware of John L. Dube, the editor of *Ilanga lase Natal*, who founded a commune not far from the Phoenix Settlement, and who went on to play such an important role in the establishment of the South African Native National Congress in 1912, later the ANC. Gandhi also travelled in 1909 to London on the same liner that carried W.P. Schreiner who defended the African cause before the Imperial authorities, and about whom he spoke highly. Gandhi, in common with the Indian leaders generally, not only harboured racial prejudice against Africans, but considered them inferior. Gandhi reflected on his jail experiences with other satyagrahis, and he expressed his objection to having to share the same facilities with Africans. The prejudices against the 'Kaffirs', as he called them, show through. 'We may entertain no aversion to Kaffirs', he wrote in 1909, 'but we cannot ignore the fact that there is no common ground between them and us in the daily affairs of life.'[23]

So, except for a loose alliance with the Chinese Association in the Transvaal, in which Gandhi violated his own policy, he and the other Indian leaders did not seek out political allies from among the other blacks. This was perhaps typical of sojourner politics, an aspect of which was that the Indian leaders of the NIC and BIA, most of whom were born in India, did not think of South Africa as their home. With friends and family in India, they made regular trips there to look after their vested interests. They had left India but had not quite abandoned her, and still looked upon that country as the 'motherland'. This must in part explain why they could not identify with 'children of the soil' in South Africa.

### Direct Challenge: Satyagraha

The satyagraha campaign started in the Transvaal in 1907. The solemn oath that 3 000 Indians took in the Empire Theatre in September 1906, was put to the test when the British government gave assent to the Transvaal Asiatic Registration Act (No. 2) of 1907. This law required Indians to register anew, giving all ten finger impressions as a form of identification. 'Honour' demanded that Indians could not degrade themselves in this fashion, the satyagrahis said. Another law, the Transvaal Immigration Registration Act (No. 15) of 1908, also became a target. Act 15 introduced a literacy test for would-be Indian immigrants. Those who qualified to enter, would still need to register under Act 2 of 1907.

It was under these circumstances that the campaign began. Indians undertook to refuse registration, and thus courted arrest. Educated Indians were to enter the Transvaal from Natal and offer themselves up for arrest by violating the laws. Below is a chronological outline of the campaign:

*September 1906 – August 1907* After the oath had been taken, work began in earnest to prepare for possible passive resistance. Gandhi and H. O. Ally undertook a trip to London in 1906, on behalf of the BIA, to attempt to persuade the British government to disallow the Asiatic Registration Act. Their mission was successful.

*September 1907 – January 1908* Royal assent was given to exactly the same law, Act 2 of 1907, passed once again by the Transvaal legislature, and the law became official. The passive resistance campaign began enthusiastically. Many, including Gandhi, went to jail.

*February 1908 – September 1908* A compromise was reached between Gandhi and Smuts in January 1908 to the effect that if Indians registered voluntarily, Act 2 of 1907 would be repealed. There was much misunderstanding of Gandhi's motives, and the Indian leader was assaulted by Mir Alam.

*August 1908 – May 1911* The compromise came undone, and the passive resistance campaign was resumed in August 1908. At the height of the campaign many were prepared to go to jail, and nearly 3 000 did. But by 1910 the campaign had lost much support. During this period,

Gandhi sought out other allies as the merchant base of his support eroded. By this time, the Union of South Africa had come into being; Gandhi had gone to London on a second BIA deputation in 1909, and had come back without success. Smuts, then the Minister of Interior, and Gandhi, reached a provisional agreement. Both were masters at the game of buying time for themselves.

*May 1911 – August 1913*   During this period of provisional agreement (extended by mutual consent), Smuts undertook to repeal Act 2 of 1907, and in its place to introduce a Union immigration bill. When the bill became law, Gandhi found the Union Immigration Act unsatisfactory in that it took away rights that had previously existed. However, Gandhi did not rush into a resumption of the campaign. He gave Smuts many opportunities to change the law, but none was taken. Meanwhile, the Cape Supreme Court ruled in the Searle decision that marriages conducted according to Hindu and Muslim rites had no legal validity.

*September 1913 – January 1914*   The campaign was resumed in September 1913 with the involvement of indentured Indians. Thousands of them went on strike, and joined the campaign. On 6 November 1913, over 2 000 indentured Indians undertook the Great March from Natal into the Transvaal.

*14 January 1914 – 26 June 1914*   Smuts was under pressure to reach settlement with Gandhi because of a white railway workers' strike at the time. A commission was appointed; an agreement was reached; and it was formalised in the Indian Relief Act of 26 June 1914. By this law: the £3 tax was repealed; the status of Indian wives was restored; the right of entry of South African-born Indians into the Cape was restored; the racial reference to the immigration law in the Orange Free State was eliminated. The government promised a fair and liberal administration of the laws affecting Indians.

*The Search for Imperial Brotherhood*

The sequence of events given above in outline does not reflect the complexity of the movement. As a moral crusade in search of the truth, the movement had a characteristic Gandhian stamp. The means by which the battle was to be fought were as important as the goals. *Satyagraha*, that is 'truth force,' implied maintaining a high moral level. Non-violence (*ahimsa*) in word and deed was important; and the 'enemy' should never be embarrassed by falsehood. He should be given ample opportunity to see the wrongfulness of his ways. Hence, it was necessary to keep the adversary informed about goals; and if an opportunity arose for arriving at an honourable compromise, it should be taken. Not everybody understood the Gandhian approach, or cared for it if they did. Gandhi's leadership was challenged and even rejected. This development was both the cause and the consequence of the political growth and maturity that occurred in Gandhi. After being abandoned by the commercial élite, Gandhi searched for other allies, and discovered mass support among people he had largely ignored up to 1913, namely the indentured Indians.

In order to see how this happened, it is necessary to examine developments in the NIC. Even before the satyagraha campaign proper had started in September 1907, the NIC had expressed support, and had appealed to its members for funds.[24] At an NIC meeting on 29 July 1907, some three months after this appeal, Gandhi told those present that everybody stood to benefit by the campaign that was anticipated. 'If we pass the test,' he said, 'Indians in all parts of the world will reap the benefit.'[25] Prominent NIC members stepped forward to participate actively in the campaign. Dawad Mahomed, Parsee Rustomjee, M.C. Anglia, and S.J. Randeria were among the people who came forward to be arrested in the Transvaal.[26] Gandhi was, of course, grateful to them, but he wanted the NIC to play a much more active role in Natal itself. For example, he thought that the organisation should boycott the Permit Office in Durban.[27] Apparently, this did not happen, nor did any other form of direct help materialise. The NIC, it appears, was not willing to expand the campaign in Natal in the way Gandhi suggested.

In the Transvaal, the main centre of the action, Gandhi found strong support in the beginning from the BIA, a great many of whose Muslim members were affiliated to the Hamidia Islamic Society (HIS). Gujarati hawkers, Hindus and Muslims, gave the campaign strong support. They were among the three thousand who filled the Transvaal jails between 1907 and 1909. On the other hand, 'Kanemias' and 'Memons' proved troublesome. The Pathans, one of whose members had assaulted Gandhi, did not quite trust Gandhi. Two Pathans also attacked Essop Mian, the BIA president. Many Indians secretly took out permits. Gandhi persisted. Picket lines were organised outside the Permit Office; and the *Indian Opinion* kept up the pressure. The satyagrahis were given prominence in its columns and praised; and those who took out permits had their names printed. Ram Sundar Pundit, the first resister to go to jail, was lionised when he was arrested in 1907; when, however, early in 1908 he fled to India rather than go to jail again, the *Indian Opinion* was not kind to him. 'Having meanly betrayed the people of Germiston, his community, himself and his family, he fled like a coward in fear of imprisonment,' said the Gujarati column.[28]

The key to understanding the initial organisational success of the campaign is in the nature of the Indian bodies at the time and their peculiar relationships with each other through overlapping membership. Thus, for example, the BIA's leaders were also the leaders of HIS; those who served NIPU could well have been members of the NIC, the Durban Indian Society (DIS), and the Young Men's Catholic Society (YMCS). Hindus could have been members of the NIC as well as the Hindu Young Men's Association (HYMA), or the Sanatan Ved Dharma Sabha. Many Muslims in the Anjuman Islam were also affiliated to the NIC. There were also the Parsis who belonged to the Zoroastrian Anjuman, some of whose members were in the NIC as well. In February 1910, the Kathiawad Arya Society in Durban organised a meeting at which Gandhi explained the movement in the Transvaal. Some of the leading Muslim supporters were present at this meeting organised by a Hindu group. In another instance, the Brahman Mandal representing the priest caste of ten regions in Natal, met in 1912 at the Umgeni Hindu Temple in Durban to support Gandhi's campaign. There are other organisations with a cultural and/or social orientation: the Patidar Association in the Transvaal, and the Tamil Benefit Society (TBS). There are many other organisations about which little is known except that they had narrow caste-related interests. A lot more needs to be known about local organisations among Kanemias, Memons, Pathans, and Gujarati Hindu caste groups.

While Gandhi may have used one or two of these for the initiation of the campaign, as was the case with the BIA, he shrewdly moved across all the bodies that had interlocking membership. In that way he was covering all groups along class, religious, and cultural lines. Thus it was, that, as he began losing merchant support in the BIA and NIC, he moved to the Patidar Association and the Tamil Benefit Society; and in Natal he moved closer to NIPU and CBIA. He hoped to secure their support by addressing issues that concerned them. This certainly helped. As he said about the Tamils in April 1910, they had 'been keeping the flag of satyagraha flying'.[29]

By the end of 1910, however, Gandhi realised that the fire had gone out of the campaign. The older groups, certainly bodies like the BIA and NIC, dominated by the more substantial merchants, no longer supported the movement. Other groups like NIPU and the CBIA sustained the campaign for a while. But he needed the support of newer elements. The provisional agreement made in 1911 gave him enough time to think about ways to revitalise the campaign if it became necessary. And when it became apparent to him by June 1913 that the resumption of the campaign was inevitable, he determined to incorporate the indentured Indians. His weapon was the £3 tax. He selected the stalwarts among the satyagrahis, his faithful soldiers, to canvass for support among the indentured Indians through strike action. He followed up with visits to talk to the Indian workers. The strike started at the Newcastle colliery, and from there spread to other sectors over

a wide region: railways, sugar refineries, and sugar plantations. As many as fifteen to twenty thousand eventually joined
the action. A most dramatic moment occurred when over two
thousand of the strikers participated in the Great March from
Natal to the Transvaal.[30] The mass support Gandhi had hoped
for materialised at last.

Why did the indentured Indians, lacking in mature political
and worker consciousness, come out so forcefully for Gandhi?
Swan explained it in terms of their deference to a leader who
had a higher social status, and of their high expectations of
him. J.D. Beall and M.D. North-Coombes located the mass
action in the context of the developing relationship between
workers and employers. The exploitation of workers by
employers had created resentment; and, in the minds of the
indentured Indians, there was no strict separation between the
employers and the colonial state in terms of who should be
blamed for the £3 tax.[31] While the whole issue awaits further
research, it is clear that the answer lies firstly, in Gandhi's
enlarged vision which included the indentured Indians as part
of the satyagraha strategy, secondly, in the perceptions of the
workers however they may have been informed, and thirdly, in
Gandhi's ability to recognise and exploit the opportunity to
mobilise the masses.

The erosion of support among the commercial élite in Natal
and the Transvaal was apparent by the end of 1913. Gandhi
denied this in an interview with the *Transvaal Leader* on
30 September 1913. He averred that there had been merchants
present at a recent meeting. Besides, even if some refused to
go to jail, most of them were willing to help financially.
Numbers did not matter, Gandhi said, even if there was only
one passive resister, the truth would prevail in the end.[32] In
spite of Gandhi's denial, the breach was a reality. At an NIC
meeting in Durban on 19 October 1913, the two secretaries,
M.C. Anglia and Dada Osman, tendered their resignations.
They attacked Gandhi in a statement calling his entire twenty
years of work 'worthless' and indeed inimical to Indian interests. They also accused Gandhi of having enticed Indians into

'slavery'. This was strong language. The meeting refused to accept the secretaries' resignation, which forced Gandhi and his supporters to withdraw from the meeting. They met at Parsee Rustomjee's home, and there formed a new body, the Natal Indian Association (NIA). Dawad Mahomed, formerly the NIC head, was chosen as president. Omar Haji Amod Jhavery became the secretary. The NIA resolved to support the passive resistance campaign.[33] So, at a critical point in the campaign, the NIC withdrew its support.

Gandhi blamed this on 'side issues',[34] but it is clear that the disgruntled NIC members felt alienated from him. They did not like the direction of the campaign, and forced a showdown with Gandhi and his supporters in the hope of gaining control over the movement. The feud continued. When the government appointed the Solomon Commission, the NIA advised its boycott because it found two of its three members unacceptable.[35] The NIC, on the other hand, decided at its meeting on 28 January 1914, to submit evidence to it. Gandhi dismissed their gesture in a cable to Gokhale, explaining their behaviour as being of little local significance. The meeting had been 'engineered by men who were opposed to the passive resistance at the very beginning of the struggle'.[36] Anglia and Osman testified on behalf of the NIC. P.S. Aiyar and Sooker, no identification provided, also gave evidence. Writing in *Indian Opinion*, Gandhi seemed to think that all their testimonies lacked depth. Anglia, speaking for all Indians, spoke only of immigration and trade issues; and Aiyar and Sooker gave evidence 'without thinking'.[37]

What was the cause of the split? Recent scholars have attributed it primarily to ideological differences between the merchants, on the one hand, who were generally self-interestedly pragmatic, and Gandhi, on the other, who by 1913 was driven more by moral imperatives that included an enlarged vision of the welfare of all Indians in South Africa than by narrow concerns.[38] Yet the division is not as categorical as one might imagine. Anglia and Osman, who opposed Gandhi in 1913, were among those merchants who had given their solid

support to the campaign earlier; and people like Dawad
Mahomed and Jhavery continued their support of Gandhi
beyond 1913. Parsee Rustomjee's support never wavered. If
wealthy Indians were generally supportive of Gandhi's campaign, even during its broadened phase, it means that they
were at least aware of its political significance beyond their
narrow self-interest. They may well have accepted the notion
that the struggle should be seen as affecting all Indians. The
split, then, can be viewed, in part if not in its entirety, as a
clash of styles in leadership and organisation and of personali-
ties. Anglia and Aiyar were both testy individuals who saw
themselves as leaders; and they disliked Gandhi's style of
doing things which they perceived as autocratic. Gandhi was
faulted, for example, for relying too heavily on whites like
H.S.L. Polak. Under these circumstances, it was easy to
accuse Gandhi of having been 'worthless' and harmful to
Indian interests, as Anglia and Osman did.

The agreement reached on 14 January 1914, between Gand-
hi and Smuts, no doubt gave the NIA some credibility. At an
NIA mass meeting eleven days later at which three thousand
Indians were present, the agreement was explained. While
Gandhi's NIA supporters were happy, others remained critical.
H.O. Ally, a former BIA president who had accompanied
Gandhi to London, was dissatisfied with the application of the
word 'final' to the agreement. 'With what right or face would
any Indian organisation apply to General Smuts in the future?'
he asked. The Hamidia Islamic Society and the Hamidad
Society passed resolutions on 31 March 1914, to the effect that
Gandhi and his friends had no authority to act for them.
Questions were also raised about a sum of £1 200 in passive
resistance money having been used for *Indian Opinion*. As
Habib Motan said, the newspaper was only registered in
Gandhi's name; Gandhi did not own it.[39]

Gandhi was to leave South Africa later in the year never to
return. His work was done, he believed. He called the Indian
Relief Act a 'Magna Charta'. If by that he meant that there was
irreversibility in the rights of Indians thereby acknowledged,

he was mistaken. The Indian position would deteriorate in the decades ahead. However, he probably meant that the Relief Act was a good foundation upon which to build. It represented success, limited as it was; and it came in the last phase of the campaign during which the support of the colonial-born élite and the indentured Indians was crucially important. Gandhi's reliance on these elements showed his growth from the time he had helped to establish the NIC twenty years earlier.

Gandhi's enduring legacy was that he created 'Indianness'. By seeking to unite the diverse elements from India, he helped a new identity emerge. He reassured the whites by creating distinctions between the 'Indian' and the 'Kaffir' other as the true savage. Indians came from a civilisation that was consistent with all the colonial markers of acceptability. The 'Kaffir' was the real source of white fears. It is remarkable how much of this thinking continued in the 1920s and 1930s, and even beyond, although some of the racial crudeness disappeared. It suited the white power as it reiterated 'Indianness' and 'Indians' as a separate racial category. This racialisation became embedded in South African politics, much as it did in the United States, as Omi and Winant pointed out in their work.[40]

The NIC was left in some disarray in 1914. Not much is known about its activity in the next several years until it was revived in the 1920s.

## CHAPTER 3

# Division and Disillusion

## 1920s to 1940s

The NIC as an organisation was intact when Gandhi departed from South Africa, but it disappeared from sight during the war years. Towards the end of the war, when instances of anti-Indianism were increasing, consideration was given to reviving the body. On 7 September 1919, the South African Indian Conference took place in Cape Town, with representatives from all the provinces. The Durban contingent of twenty-three included M.C. Anglia who had disagreed with Gandhi in 1913–14.[1] Out of this meeting was to emerge the Natal Committee of the South African Indian Conference.

A year later some individuals in Natal considered that the province should have a formal body as an affiliate of the national organisation. The NIA and the CBIA were operational, but the sentiment was in favour of a revival of the NIC which retained the Gandhian connection and still had assets.[2] A group consisting of P.K. Naidoo and others constituted itself as the Congress Resuscitation Committee (CRC) in December 1920. E.M. Paruk became the chairman while V.S.C. Pather and S. Emammally were appointed as secretaries. The CRC vigorously set about the task of re-forming the NIC by advertising a general meeting, distributing subscription forms at a fee of 10s. 6d., and in other ways canvassing for support. A meeting took place on 6 March 1921 in Durban. Ismail Gora was elected as president. There were six vice-presidents. A. Christopher and Manilal M. Gandhi were the joint secretaries; and O.H.A. Jhavery and V.S.C. Pather were the joint treasurers. In addition, there was a twenty-four-person committee.[3]

The names of the executive members suggest a desire on the part of the organisers to ensure that a wide cross-section of Indians would be represented on the NIC. And, of course, there was a strong Gandhi connection: Gandhi's son as well as those with whom he had close ties, like Christopher and Jhavery, were included. The subscription fee was significantly reduced to attract more members; and the former NIC objective, namely to promote good relations between whites and Indians as a way to improve the lot of the Indians, was retained.[4]

In the next annual general meeting on 23 April 1922, Amod Bayat was elected to the NIC presidency, a position he was to occupy for much of the 1920s. He was sixty years old then, and reputed to be a good businessman. During the 1920s, the whole country 'throbbed with diabolic anti-Indianism', to quote P.S. Joshi.[5] Old issues such as trade licences, immigration restrictions, and general segregation resurfaced. The state, especially after the Pact government came into being in 1924, appeared deliberately intent on making it clear to the Indians, through legislation, that their lives would be made intolerable if they chose to remain in South Africa. Two bills in 1924 and 1925, namely the Class Areas Bill and the Areas Reservation Bill, threatened residential and trade segregation. The Colour Bar Act and the Liquor Act also affected the Indians adversely. On the local and provincial levels too, discriminatory laws rapidly made their appearance. Natal, for example, took away the municipal franchise from Indians in 1924. There was generally a concerted effort on the part of Indians actively to resist and oppose these measures.

The NIC organised mass meetings as and when the need arose throughout these years. It submitted petitions, and was very active in organising protest meetings.[6] The South African Indian Conference formally became the South African Indian Congress (SAIC) in 1923. The SAIC co-ordinated the campaign in the three provinces through its affiliates, among which the NIC played the most influential role. The SAIC planned to use the influence of India in their fight, especially the Indian National Congress (INC). It established official contact with the INC, and used the services of people like Sarojini Naidu and C.F. Andrews, both of whom were well connected with M.K. Gandhi. Naidu, for example, was elected to the SAIC presidency in 1924, a position she continued to hold until 1929; and Andrews made many trips to help establish round table conferences. Gandhi's influence was thus considerable in the 1920s. As secretary of the All-India Congress Committee, Jawaharlal Nehru (the future prime minister of India) prepared a paper in 1927 entitled 'A Foreign Policy for India', and his strong defence of the rights of Indians abroad enhanced India's role in South Africa.

In thus seeking to use India's influence, the SAIC opted for the imperial route towards finding solutions. In 1925, the SAIC sent a deputation to India specifically to protest the Class Areas Bill. Among the deputation members were high-ranking NIC officials.[7] The deputation met with the Viceroy of India, and presented its case at protest meetings in Bombay, Madras, and Calcutta. The Government of India, in turn, sent the Paddison Deputation in 1926, which paved the way for a formal round table conference between the governments of India and South Africa towards the end of 1926. Out of this was to emerge the Cape Town Agreement.[8]

**The Cape Town Agreement**
The Cape Town Agreement of 1927 was a logical outcome of the policy followed by the South African Indian leaders of the time. With Amod Bayat as president, the NIC was firmly in control of the politics of Natal Indians. The organisation had expanded to reach many parts of Natal; it had a positive bank balance thanks to a contribution of £1 000 made by the Imperial Citizenship Association. Its leaders were firmly behind the empire. When the Prince of Wales visited Durban, the NIC officially welcomed him although, to its credit, it refused to participate in segregated ceremonies. The prince visited 110 Field Street, which was then the official headquarters of the NIC.[9] The NIC looked to India to achieve a status of equality for Indians; it also celebrated significant

events in India, and honoured and paid respects to leaders in India.

Agreement was reached at Cape Town in two broad areas, namely, repatriating Indians voluntarily through a subsidised scheme, and pursuing a policy of 'upliftment' for those Indians who remained behind in South Africa. A diplomatic representative of the Government of India, known at first as the Agent, was to oversee the repatriation scheme, and generally take up issues that concerned South African Indians, but in no specific sense was he their spokesperson. The SAIC, which was denied participation in the conference, held an emergency meeting to endorse the approach. It held out high hopes. 'Our aim right from the commencement,' said the official SAIC statement, 'was to secure the holding of the Round Table Conference for a[n] honourable and lasting settlement of the Indian question.'[10]

The NIC, whose members were highly placed in the SAIC, shared these expectations. Even if the dates of its annual general meetings usually overshot by many months, it could boast several achievements: the NIC had added a Social Service Committee and the Indian Child Welfare Society in 1928, and played a role in the formation of the Indian Trade Union Congress. The 1931 NIC report referred to report-back meetings in branches like Clairwood, Sydenham, Mayville, Umgeni, Tongaat, Stanger, Darnell, and Pietermaritzburg.[11] But there were sources of division and disunity, as will be seen below.

**Sources of Division**
There were already rumblings in South African Indian politics when the agency was created. Some well-placed individuals felt that the repatriation scheme, even though it was voluntary, was an unnecessary concession made by the wealthy elements at the expense of the poor. Those who bore the onus of accepting the scheme would probably feel no need to repatriate themselves under its workings. The appearance of the Natal Indian Vigilance Association (NIVA) in 1926, P.S. Aiyar being

one of the founding members, signified unhappiness with the NIC. The South African Indian Federation (SAIF), however, came into being in 1927 in opposition to the SAIC specifically over features of the Cape Town Agreement which it saw as unacceptable. The SAIF disappeared after a couple of years, but the general atmosphere of criticism within which it was established continued into the 1930s. As more and more issues surfaced, and as the disabilities imposed on Indians mounted, the agency's usefulness came seriously into question; and the approach of the officials in control of the SAIC was increasingly discredited, and with it, that of the NIC as well.[12] Three specific sources of the division are explored below.

*Colonisation*

Religion, language, and class differences have always been present in NIC politics. Those with passenger origins often considered themselves better pedigreed than Indians with indentured origins. The passenger Indians came mainly from western parts of India where Gujarati was spoken, and used the term 'Girmitiyas' to refer dismissively to indentured Indians; in the post-indentured period other terms were used with similar irreverence: 'Culcuttias' for Bhojpuri-speakers from the Ganges valley, and 'Madrassis' for Tamil- and Telugu-speakers from the southern parts of India. Not infrequently, the term 'banias' was reserved for the Gujarati-speaking traders to suggest that they were grasping individuals not to be trusted. The NIC was supposed to be a secular body, and religion, language and class were meant to be of no consequence. But in reality they did matter. Gujarati-speaking Muslim merchants always appeared to be in control of the organisation. Communal passions between Hindus and Muslims could easily be enflamed, as they were, for example, when Agent-General Sir Syed Raza Ali married Miss Ponoo Veloo Sammy in January 1936. It seriously affected Indian politics which had generally been tolerant of religious differences, and led to the resignation of the entire NIC executive. J. W. Godfrey, who was president of the NIC and of the SAIC, resigned from both positions. The NIC's joint secretaries, one of the treasurers, four vice-presidents, and thirteen of the committee members also resigned. There were resignations from the SAIC as well.[13]

In the colonisation issue, there was a mixture of all the divisive elements. In addition, there was also the class dimension. It caused a serious rift in Natal's Indian politics, and brought about a major crisis in leadership in the NIC and the SAIC. The roots of the conflict lay in the Cape Town Agreement.

The South African government was disappointed that only a couple of thousand Indians had elected to return to India under the assisted emigration scheme. It made known its disappointment at the second round table conference in 1933, and the Indian delegation suggested voluntary colonisation of South Africa's Indians, largely with the view to keeping the Cape Town Agreement alive. A commission of inquiry was to be appointed to look into the possibility of shipping off Indians to a suitable country. The idea had been in the air ever since 1921, when the government had tried, without success, to appoint a deputation to visit British Guiana to check out its suitability for relocating Indians. The SAIC, of which the NIC was a constituent body, agreed to participate in the enquiry believing quite naively that to participate was not to agree to the commission's recommendations. Many Indians did not see it that way. Out of this controversy was to emerge the Colonial Born and Settler Indian Association (CBSIA).

The CBSIA was made up mainly of Indians who were descended from indentured workers. Many of them were first-generation South Africans and did not consider India as their home. In their opinion, the SAIC had erred in its decision, and had thus forfeited the right to speak for them. The CBSIA's prime initiator and also its first president was Albert Christopher. Christopher had been secretary of the Colonial Born Indian Association (f. 1911); and had supported the final phase of the satyagraha campaign. In 1914, he wrote a short article in the *Golden Number*, a commemorative issue of the

## Division and Disillusion

*Indian Opinion*, which reflected on the satyagraha campaign. Since immigration from India had been stopped, the resolution of the Indian question would gradually fall upon the shoulders of South African-born Indians in whom, he wrote, there was 'material worthy of a part of the structure of South Africa'.[14] A trained lawyer, Christopher had been in Congress politics ever since qualifying. He was SAIC president in 1930. P. R. Pather was another founding member, who considered himself a 'progressive' at that stage, but whose politics were to change in the 1940s.[15]

The CBSIA found a strong supporter in Manilal M. Gandhi, M. K. Gandhi's second son who had been charged by his father with the responsibility of running the *Indian Opinion*. At the inaugural meeting of the CBSIA, Christopher accused the SAIC of not working for the benefit of all Indians. When faced with a crisis, the SAIC was willing to sacrifice the poor and the illiterate in their ranks, he continued. Christopher roundly criticised the agency for having superseded the Indian political organisations. He didn't want the agency to speak for people like him. 'The time has now come,' Christopher said, 'for us who were born in this country and represent the fourth and fifth generations . . . and . . . who have adopted this country as our homes . . . [to] face our position . . . fairly and squarely.' The CBSIA's ideal was to work for economic equality and for 'common brotherhood'.[16]

The SAIC was understandably defensive about its participation in the colonisation issue, and reiterated at an emergency conference that the organisation was in no way bound to accept the proposals coming out of the enquiry. S. R. Naidoo was appointed to participate in the Colonisation Commission, the work of which was begun on 28 July 1933 and completed seven months later on 3 February 1934. A report was issued in June 1934, which recommended the following countries as likely places to which some of South Africa's Indian population of 196 400 could be resettled: British North Borneo, British New Guinea, and British Guiana. The Indians were horrified that the commission could consider dumping them in distant places they had not even heard of. The SAIC quickly distanced itself from the proposal by rejecting it, though S.R. Naidoo had given his assent to the report.[17]

The CBSIA vented its anger at the agency's involvement by sending a cable to the All-India Congress Committee requesting it to disapprove the appointment of the next agent-general on the 'principal ground [that the] agency in South Africa [was] impotent in the absence of [the] Indians' freedom'.[18]

Although the CBSIA came into being in response to the single issue of colonisation, its creation was nevertheless symptomatic of the SAIC's perceived neglect of the poorer classes of Indians. Its inaugural conference promised to attend to the needs of these elements. The CBSIA, which drew its support mainly from Indians in Natal, seriously undermined the NIC. But the organisation promised more than it could deliver. It did not even live up to its own expectations. References to this organisation disappear by the end of the 1940s as many of its members found their way back to the SAIC or its affiliate, the NIC. New differences emerged, and these tended to divide the NIC and a new organisation, the Natal Indian Association (NIA).

By 1938, the leadership of the CBSIA and the NIC gradually moved towards amalgamating both bodies into the NIA. While there was talk of unity, there appeared to be a scramble on both sides to gain support among wavering members. The NIC seemed to have the edge as the CBSIA experienced wholesale defection from among its ranks, especially in its Pietermaritzburg branch. The NIC began a monthly newsletter in 1938; and its annual meeting was marked by thoroughness of preparation. In any event, the two organisations were ready for amalgamation towards the end of 1939. An amended constitution not differing much in essential matters was drawn up.[19] A mass meeting of ten thousand people on 8 October 1939 at Curries Fountain sealed the amalgamation. The name, NIA, was accepted formally, although some were unhappy at the dropping of NIC.[20] The unity process was hardly over, when a new issue created further dissension: the outcry

## *Division and Disillusion*

over Indian 'penetration' into white areas in Durban and the Indian responses.

### *The Nationalist Bloc, the War, and NEUF*

Even as the CBSIA and the NIC merged into the NIA, there were individuals who did not quite agree with official organisational politics. Those within the ranks of the NIC who did not like the merger, wished to keep the body alive. So even with the merger in place, the NIC continued to exist as a separate body. There were, as before, two bodies competing with each other. Within the NIA itself, there was division. A group calling itself the Nationalist Bloc (NB) disagreed on matters of substance with the official leadership in the NIA. In the Transvaal, a similar group had emerged calling itself the Nationalist Group (NG). Both the NB and the NG consisted of young individuals who were uniformly much less willing to compromise on most issues. They were active in trade union organisations, were members of the SACP, or used forums such as the Liberal Study Group to articulate alternative approaches. They were generally imbued with revolutionary fervour.

Among the members of the NB were H.A. Naidoo, George Singh, C.I. Amra, P.M. Harry, D.A. Seedat, George Ponnen, and Dr G.M. Naicker. Some, for example Amra, Ponnen, and Naidoo, had been active in the Natal Youth Council since its establishment in 1937.[21] In the Transvaal, the NG consisted of people like Dr Y.M. Dadoo, S.B. Mehd, and I.A. Cachalia who seriously disagreed with the official leadership of the TIC, mainly over the right kind of response to make when the Transvaal Asiatic Land and Trading Act of 1939 was passed. The NG became stronger but, mainly on the advice of M.K. Gandhi, it did not resort to passive resistance to fight the 1939 land law.[22]

The two groups also disagreed on the issue of South Africa's participation in the Second World War. The NIA, NIC and TIC leadership had offered their support unconditionally. Dadoo, who was a member of the SACP, followed the party line and denounced the war's imperialist objectives. He went to jail for his anti-war utterances.[23] Even those who were not SACP members identified strongly with India's struggle for independence, and believed that the Allied nations should not be supported until they clearly announced their intentions of giving freedom to all colonially subjected peoples. The NIC itself opposed India's unconditional support for the Allied war effort. Within the NIA, the NB members who opposed the war were expelled. They were: B.A. Maharaj, D.A. Seedat, H.A. Naidoo, George Singh, P.M. Harry, Dr K. Goonam, and Dr G.M. Naicker. It did not deter the NB members from demonstrating outside the recruiting offices in Durban; and D.A. Seedat went to jail for his beliefs.[24] Many SACP members reversed their position when the Soviet Union aligned itself with the Allied nations in 1941.

Both the NB and the NG considered that the official NIC and TIC approach to South African Indian issues was much too accommodating to the white power structure. That approach relied heavily on the imperial connection, as well as on the influence of white moderates, among whom would be people who considered themselves 'liberals'. V.S.S. Sastri, the first diplomatic agent under the Cape Town Agreement, had hoped to use the influence of white liberals to improve the lot of the Indians, and towards this end he had started the Indo-European councils. But neither the imperial connection, nor the white liberal influence helped to improve the position of the Indians in South Africa significantly. So it was that the dissident elements among the Indians turned to the idea of an alliance with other blacks. The Non-European United Front (NEUF) was the organisation to which they gravitated.

Race and ethnicity defined the membership of black political organisations in the early days. In reaction to the exclusivist politics of an emerging white supremacist ethos, black leaders themselves used race as a core around which to organise their politics. They presupposed some kind of unity of interest within a racial classification. It was, of course, not true that interests fell neatly into such a categorisation. There was much diversity of class and culture within all groups. It was an organising principle imposed by the dominant group which saw clear benefits in a fragmented black opposition. The legacy of separate ethnically oriented approaches established in Gandhi's day continued in the period after the First World War.

The first among the black leaders to make a serious effort to unite the organisations was Dr Abdul Abdurahman. Born in 1872, Abdurahman spent seven years abroad from 1888 to 1895, during which time he qualified as a doctor at the University of Glasgow and undertook post-graduate research in London. He was elected to the Cape Town city council in 1904, a position he held until his death in 1940 with a break during the years from 1913 to 1915. In 1914, he was elected to the Cape provincial council, a seat he held until 1940. In 1902, Abdurahman founded the African Political (later People's) Organisation. He was one of the delegates who went to India as part of the SAIC delegation. Soon after his return he advocated the formation of a broad front of black organisations.

In June 1927, Abdurahman took the initiative in organising the first Non-European Unity Front (NEUF) conference. There was great pressure from the government on individual members not to associate with 'extremists'. In his opening address, Abdurahman denounced efforts by the government to divide people into 'watertight compartments', and its continued denial of political rights to blacks. He continued:

> To the Malay the government said: "We will make you different from the Asiatics," and to the Coloured man: "You will get the status of the white man." Some poor deluded fools already walked about the streets as if they were white and really better than all others.[25]

There were 114 delegates at the first NEUF conference. Thirteen organisations were represented, among them the ANC, ICU, and the SAIC.[26] While the two official SAIC members supported black unity, they pointed out that their organisation's constitution prevented them from supporting formal resolutions adopted at the conference.

There were other such conferences in which Abdurahman took a leading part. Cape Town hosted one in January 1930; and a third was held in Bloemfontein a year later. Neither the SAIC nor the NIC was represented at either of the two conferences. There was one more NEUF meeting in April 1939. In the absence of Abdurahman, his daughter Zainunissa ('Cissie') Gool presided over a conference marked by divisiveness.[27] In any event, Indian political organisations had, since the 1927 Cape Town Agreement, opted for the round table conference as a mechanism by which to resolve issues dealing with Indians. The presence of the diplomatic representative under the agreement merely added confusion to the scene. His efforts to speak on behalf of South Africa's Indians was resented by the local Indian population. Furthermore, the interests of the Government of India were not the same as those of Indians in South Africa. The intervention of the agency merely delayed the process by which Indians could search for solutions in the South African political context.

NEUF had support in Durban among the NB members. At a conference on 26 November 1939, the broad-based opposition of all blacks was endorsed as the most effective way to fight segregation.[28] The NIC officials balked at the idea; and in this they had at least had the backing of M.K. Gandhi, who even in 1939 believed, as he told the Revd S.S. Thema of the D.R. Mission in Johannesburg, that it would be a mistake for Indians to join the Africans politically because they would be 'pooling together not strength but weakness'. Indians were not regarded as a 'menace' by the whites. The Africans were bound to resist because they had been robbed of their inheritance. Gandhi concluded, 'Yours is a bigger issue. It ought not to be mixed up with that of the Indians.'[29]

S.R. Naidoo, a top-ranking NIC and SAIC member, thought very much along the same lines. Writing in *Indian Views*, he said that Indians would be throwing away the advantage of their 'resources' if they allied themselves with the Africans. (It is possible that he meant civilisation and culture by 'resources'.) The Indians had the ability to turn a 'weakness into strength', he continued. Naidoo pointed to the mutual understanding promoted by Indo-European and Euro-Bantu councils. He concluded, 'Nothing should be done to create this feeling of fear or suspicion [that is, of 'threat to White civilisation'].' Hawa W. Ahmed, a NEUF supporter, responded by saying that the 'dazzling garden parties that the Indians had organised for their liberal white friends for the past 30 years had brought them nothing'.[30]

All of this was related to the making of a decision as to the best strategy that Indians should be using to fight segregation. The NB and NG members invariably favoured the taking of a direct-action approach, which included passive resistance. Such action, proposed by Dadoo and his supporters in 1939, was averted only on the advice of Gandhi. But they were deeply unhappy about the assurances that the NIC and TIC leaders gave to appease whites in their fear of having the white parliament pass discriminatory laws. The assurances, intended to preempt such legislation, amounted to self-segregation, and this the Indian militants were not prepared to accept. NEUF's role was taken over in the early 1940s by the Marxist-oriented Non-European Unity Movement (NEUM), but the NIC leadership went through the motions in 1943 of seeking to work with it without really being serious about joining a common black front. NEUM held out hopes for more success under the new NIC leadership after 1945, but it moved instead to an alliance with the ANC.[31]

*Self-Imposed Segregation*
The NIA executive, among whom were CBSIA leaders such as Christopher and Pather, was in the process of formulating a stand on the penetration issue. Some of the NIC leaders did not approve of the stand, and instead of disbanding the organisation so as to create one unified body, revived it. Hajee E.M. Paruk served as acting president until a new executive was elected on 18 February 1940. The newly elected executive

publicly repudiated the NIA's decision voluntarily to participate in the Lawrence Committee, then established to look into the prevention of inter-racial transfers of properties. It feared that the NIA's participation might amount to collusion in implementing segregation, and characterised the NIA as 'shamelessly' working against 'their own people'. Claiming to have two thousand supporters in Durban and another two thousand in branches in ten other Natal towns and cities, the NIC challenged the NIA's claim to represent all Natal Indians.[32] The NIC appointed a subcommittee consisting of A. I. Kajee and A. M. Moola to monitor the activities of the Indian Penetration Commission, even though it refused representation on the commission.[33] Meanwhile, the NIA produced a fairly exhaustive 180-page memorandum on land acquired by Indians in Natal since 1927, and emphatically refuted charges of penetration.[34]

Both the NIC and the NIA were soon to learn, however, that it was not participation or non-participation in commissions of enquiry that would resolve the penetration issue, but Natal's white power structure. When the earlier commission found that penetration was negligible, the Durban City Cor-poration (DCC) and the Natal Municipal Association (NMA), pushed for a new commission to reinvestigate the issue within stricter terms of reference. The later commission found 326 instances of penetration in Durban. Armed with this evidence, Natal's white politicians forced the government of J.C. Smuts to take legislative action.[35]

A bill to provide such action had already been introduced in parliament when the NIA and NIC sent deputations to Cape Town. The intervention of the Indian high commissioner led to the two bodies creating a single consultative committee which would present its opposition to the proposed law in a meeting with Smuts. This show of unity made no impression on the prime minister, but it did set the scene for the amalgamation of the two bodies. Indeed, while the Indian high commissioner cleverly used his office to press for unity – he was not prepared to accompany both delegations to the prime minister – the NIA and NIC really did not need much persuasion.[36]

On 18 July 1943, a pledge was taken by 143 members to merge the NIA into the NIC. The NIC was chosen for historical reasons as well as its greater viability. The NIA executive was added to the existing NIC structure. There were thirty vice-presidents and forty-five committee members, but NIA's J.W. Godfrey became the president, and NIC's A.M.M. Lockhat stepped down to become vice-president. P.R. Pather became one of the secretaries.[37] Whatever personal differences separated the NIA and the NIC, there were few substantive issues that distinguished the two organisations. Both opposed segregation but stopped short of challenging white supremacy. They hoped to achieve broader freedoms for Indians without, however, alienating the white power structure.

While there were few ideological differences, the dominance in the NIC of the wealthy merchant class was apparent and continued into the early 1940s, which explains why the organisation was generally pragmatic and accommodating. The operating expenses from 1939 to 1941 came to £1 338, of which two-thirds came from thirteen businessmen. NIC president E.M. Paruk's personal contribution was £200. Their financial contribution gave them enormous leverage in the organisation. It is worth studying the profiles of two individuals who played prominent roles before and after the amalgamation, and whose ideologies merged: A.I. Kajee (1896–1947) and P.R. Pather (d. 1970).

A.I. Kajee was born in India in 1896, and was first brought to South Africa in 1901. He was to return to India several times, once even as a student at Aligarh University. He tried a variety of occupations in India before returning to Durban to take up a position in Amod Bayat's firm around 1916. It was after yet another trip to India in 1921 that Kajee ventured into his own business, an agency under the name, A.I. Kajee (Pty) Ltd which was to thrive in the next two decades.[38]

Kajee entered public life in the 1920s, and was soon to establish himself in the NIC and the SAIC. His work was marked by thoroughness and efficiency. He was energetic and used his talent for memorising statistics to good advantage when arguing a case. But he was also known to be high-handed and dictatorial. In any event, by the late 1930s he had become influential in Indian politics. The mass resignations in the NIC after the agent-general's marriage helped to propel him to leadership. Kajee showed a paternalistic concern for Indians, and this included Indian labourers, although he was not inclined to identify with their rights as trade union members.[39]

His political stance was characterised by a pragmatism that involved no direct confrontation with the white authorities. Kajee accepted the Cape Town Agreement as a basis from which to secure the best possible advantages for the Indians; and if this meant compromises, he was willing to make them. Reacting to rumours about Indians being offered indirect representation in Parliament, he said in 1938, 'We do not desire to alter the political complexion of this country . . .' He was quite prepared to accept white members of Parliament representing Indians. Kajee's thinking is worth quoting in full:

> There is a community of interest between Europeans and Indians in trade, industry, professions, farming and in every phase of life, and we are quite prepared to elect Europeans and to trust them to do their best in the interest of all communities who have made this land their home and for the good of South Africa.[40]

Since his entire philosophy was to cultivate harmonious relations between the Indians and the whites, he could not accept the kind of strategy that was being promoted by NEUF. Kajee was a conservative who was also a shrewd politician. He was also well read, and politicians of all persuasions were welcome in his home. But there was a hypocritical streak in the man as well, as I.C. Meer was to discover, typified by Kajee's public and private positions on allowing Africans to attend a cinema owned by him. He did not want to exclude African patrons publicly, but had instructed his staff to do so privately.[41]

Pather, who ran in the 1940s a real estate and insurance

business in Durban, entered politics at about the same time that Kajee did. In 1928, he was joint-secretary of both the NIC and the SAIC. He left the fold of these two organisations in 1933 to help found the CBSIA, in which he remained active until 1939. But in 1939 he worked to unite the CBSIA and the NIC into the NIA; and thereafter he was involved in the process through which the NIA merged into the NIC. In both instances, he claimed the role of a 'chief architect' working for unity.[42] Whatever the differences between Pather and Kajee, they shared the basic philosophy of working closely with the white power structure. Pather was a member of the Indo-European Joint Council, and worked to create harmonious relations with the whites. It was this convergence of ideas and approaches that finally brought them together to travel along the conservative road from about the middle of 1943. Both opposed direct confrontation with the white power structure, and openly challenged their militant colleagues who advocated it.[43] The strategy of conservatives like Kajee and Pather was to keep the reins of control from the hands of the militants. But the control of the NIC gradually drifted away from them after 1943 over their handling of white accusations that Indians were infiltrating so-called white areas.

This issue, which segregationists called 'penetration', had simmered in the Transvaal and Natal in the 1930s. It resulted in the passage of the Occupation of Land (Transvaal and Natal) Restriction Act of 1943, better known as the Pegging Act. For the next three years, agreements regarding the sale, purchase, and occupation of land and properties in the Transvaal and Durban between Indians and whites needed the government's approval. The law in essence approved the pattern of segregation then in existence.

The NIC and TIC (f. 1927) leadership spoke out eloquently against the law, and were embarrassed that it should come in the midst of the Second World War, the declared aim of which was to secure freedom and justice for all. The Indian leaders supported South Africa's participation in the war over the objections of many of their supporters who regarded the

conflict as entrenching colonial rule. They had always advocated moderation despite the rhetoric they had used since
1940. 'Must we for ever', said NIC's E.M. Paruk in 1941
'remain a voiceless and voteless community, the butt of racial
Parliamentarians, a football to be kicked from side to side?'
Swami Bhawani Dayal, another leading light in the NIC,
warned in 1941 that if the attempts continued 'to filch away
any of the few remaining rights we have in Natal to own and
occupy property', he would take steps to awaken 'our Mother
country' to the realities of the situation.[44] Despite such language, the NIC and TIC leaders had opposed since 1939 the
use of passive resistance to defy segregation.[45]

Kajee ascribed the law to 'unreason' and the 'fear complex of
the European'. The word 'Indian' was like a 'red rag to the bull',
and whites were driven to 'the most extravagant follies'. But he
appeared to see politics as the main reason behind the Pegging
Act. Kajee analysed it thus, 'Such a mood is rich opportunity
for the ill-disposed politician. In such a mood, it is impossible to
reason or to argue; calm judgement flies before the hurricane of
his [the white person's] obsessions. Only in judicial conference
can facts, light, and justice have a chance of life.'[46] It was clear
to him that a compromise could be worked out if politics could
be taken out of the arena of the common white man and
woman, and away from 'ill-disposed politicians' to a forum
where reason would prevail. Similarly, militant Indians, too,
must be kept out of the process. He decided that such a forum
was the national government, whose leader, Smuts, would be
well disposed to compromises given his desire to appear fair
and just in international circles.

With this in mind, Kajee approached Smuts with a proposal
that when the Pegging Act expired, an independent board
consisting of three whites and two Indians should review all
land and property transactions between whites and Indians in
Natal. The board would consider juxtapositional residential
occupation, contiguity and so on before declaring whether a
pending transaction constituted penetration. In essence what
Kajee was proposing was to maintain residential segregation

informally on the basis of consensus. He wished to restrict only occupation of white areas, not ownership. As Kajee stated publicly, 'Compromises on both sides can achieve much. Let us not close the door to negotiation. We are prepared to occupy land in our own special areas, but we must have an equal right with the Europeans to decide which shall be those areas.'[47] Smuts liked the proposal which came to be known as the Pretoria Agreement.[48]

But the proposal came under fire from all sides. Natal's white politicians, and especially those in the DCC and NMA, had their own plans as to how residential expansion should be handled. They really wanted radially growing racial zones, and scuttled Kajee's proposal by adding amendments to it in the provincial legislature that were not acceptable even to Kajee himself. For example, they proposed a review board made up entirely of whites, and narrowed the definition of penetration to exclude contiguous acquisitions. A bitter and angry Kajee appeared before the Natal provincial council – a singular honour since no black had ever addressed the body before – and accused the whites of not being interested in resolving racial strife. The rich Indians, he said, were being made the 'bogey', the 'scapegoat' for white poverty and distress. Kajee warned that 'so long as the Indians are depressed [sic] and segregated by statutes legally imposed by the dominant group, so long will there be racial strife'. He lamented the failure of the Pretoria Agreement in a letter he wrote to Jan Hofmeyr, the Minister of the Interior on 3 April 1945. He feared that the local authorities in Natal and the Transvaal would expropriate Indian-owned land and forcibly remove Indians into segregated areas.[49]

Kajee also ran into trouble with the NIC militants. What Kajee considered 'wisdom and sound realism' was labelled as a 'reactionary' policy of self-segregation. The attack on Kajee's proposal was broadened into a blistering criticism of the NIC's leadership. The 'Kajee-Pather' group, as the old leadership came to be called, was accused of being interested only in promoting Indian businessmen. The very fact that the NIC offices were maintained on the premises of a businessman suggested to the militants that the NIC did not have 'an independent existence' separate from those interests. The NIC was a captive of business interests, and had to be freed.[50]

The militant segment of the NIC mounted an attack in the form of the Anti-Segregation Committee of Action in April 1943. A year later it was formalised into the Anti-Segregation Council (ASC). The ASC launched a campaign to oust the existing leadership. On 6 May 1944, the ASC hosted a conference at which twenty-nine organisations were represented; and at a mass meeting held at Nicol Square, it rallied several thousand Indians against the Pretoria Agreement. The ASC went beyond showing its opposition to the Kajee-Pather group. At a meeting in November 1944, it announced its own programme which was to serve as a basis of NIC politics for the next sixteen years: restoration of the franchise on the common roll, the removal of provincial barriers, the elimination of all forms of colour bar, the introduction of free and compulsory education, the redistribution of land, and the subsidisation of small market gardeners. The ASC kept up the pressure through regular mass meetings. Fearing defeat, the Kajee-Pather group postponed elections in 1945, and attempted to weaken the militants by proposing the decentralisation of the NIC. But the ASC was not to be denied success. It took the matter to the Natal Supreme Court which ordered the NIC leaders to call an annual general meeting. The NIC leaders were forced to schedule elections on 21 October 1945, but six days before that date they all resigned their offices. On 21 October 1945, the ASC was dramatically elected onto the NIC executive by over seven thousand enthusiastic supporters at the Curries Fountain sports stadium in Durban. Kajee and his cohorts did not even bother to show up. Dr G.M. (Monty) Naicker was elected to the NIC presidency, a position he would hold until 1961.[51]

While the militants captured the leadership of the NIC, the SAIC still remained in the hands of the Kajee-Pather group. In the Transvaal, the TIC had similarly been taken over, by

## *Division and Disillusion*

December 1945, by militants under the leadership of Dr Yusuf Dadoo. The death of conservative leader S.M. Nana on 8 May 1944, had helped to end the struggle for leadership that had lasted over six years. The Cape Indian Congress,which had long been one of the SAIC affiliates, remained, however, in the Kajee-Pather camp. At the national level, the struggle for leadership continued until 1948 when the SAIC came under the control of the militants. Meanwhile, the Kajee-Pather group formed a rival body called the Natal Indian Organisation (NIO) in 1948. The wrangle in the Cape continued until the CIC disaffiliated from the SAIC in 1950, when the newly established Cape Indian Assembly became an affiliate of the SAIC. In the Transvaal, too, a rival organisation emerged, namely the Transvaal Indian Organisation. In 1950, a new national body, the South African Indian Organisation (SAIO) was formed to serve the interests of the conservatives.

Kajee died in 1947, and the mantle of conservative leadership fell on Pather, A.M. Moola, and others. Pather deplored the deterioration of Indo-white relations in his reflections in 1964. He saw a 'definite trend to offend the whites at every turn'. The NIO sought to mend fences by establishing branches in Pietermaritzburg, Estcourt, Ladysmith, Glencoe, Dundee, Newcastle, Stanger, Verulam, Port Shepstone, Greytown, and Dannhauser. The conservative efforts suited the white power structure. By promoting these developments, white politicians set the parameters of Indian politics. They often worked through a conservative organisation like the NIO and thereby hoped to undermine the NIC. Even white liberals advised moderation and gradualism, which the NIO represented, and often thought the NIC militants to be 'extremists'.[52] Their faith in constitutionalism made them believe that reason would prevail in the end to produce a racially equitable society. They were certainly sympathetic to NIC militants, but it seems that they underestimated the strength of white supremacy and misunderstood the dynamics around black opposition and resistance.

Natal's Indians had a choice in the 1940s and 1950s. They

could espouse the NIC's politics of defiance under leaders who offered them a non-racial vision; or they could place their trust in the politics of quiet persuasion which placed a great deal of trust in white goodwill. The conservatives' reliance on the imperial connection had not brought tangible results. In the end, the agency was discredited, and its demise was inevitable. Indeed, some of the former agents-general like Raza Ali, called for strong action against South Africa; and High Commissioner Shafa'at Ahmad Khan had a hand in the passage of the Reciprocity Act of 1944 which imposed disabilities on white South Africans in India similar in nature to those suffered by Indians in South Africa.[53] The nationalist leaders of India saw no reason to continue working through normal diplomatic channels to help South Africa's Indians to improve their status. India's withdrawal of the high commissioner in 1946 also signalled the defeat of the conservative NIC and TIC leadership. In the late 1940s, Natal's Indians chose the NIC because its politics also restored a measure of self-respect. Whatever reservations they may have had about the NIC's new approaches, the NIO's close affiliation with the apartheid regime which denied their human worth, did little for their self-esteem.

## CHAPTER 4

# The New Leaders

## 1945 to 1961

Indians who were leaving the agricultural sector in the 1920s were gradually being absorbed into an expanding manufacturing industry in and around Durban. In 1921, there were 142 000 Indians in Natal of whom 49 688 were in the Durban municipal area. By 1936, the latter number had increased to 80 486 and then to 106 604 by 1946. In 1951, the total number of Indians stood at 147 264, which reflected a threefold increase since 1921. Greater Durban's manufacturers employed only 5 237 Indians out of a total of 25 595 in 1924. Three decades later, the number had grown to 16 827.[1]

The rapid migration of Indians into Durban and their employment in secondary industry were to have a dramatic impact on Indian politics. Many were drawn into the trade unions which were being established; between 1934 and 1945, there were at least forty-three unions with Indian members.[2] NIC leaders were quick to take advantage of the opportunity to win over the new constituents. For example, the NIC organised a mass meeting on 30 September 1931, and an unofficial labour bureau was opened. Whenever possible, the NIC leaders intervened to help resolve industrial disputes. Such intervention occurred in the case of at least two strikes, the Falkirk strike of 1937 and the Dunlop strike of 1942–43. At the time, the NIC was controlled by conservatives like Kajee, and intervention tended to be largely a matter of ethnically motivated paternalism, rather than support for the principle of workers' rights to engage in industrial action.[3] The influx of Indians into the urban centres also created pressures on housing, health services, and social welfare. The concern that something should be done about alleviating the harsh conditions in which Indians lived is reflected in the NIC agenda books of the 1940s and 1950s.

From among the ranks of the new constituents came individuals who became active in either setting up trade unions or organising workers to join them. Billy Peters at one time was a secretary of the Durban Indian Municipal Employees' Union; George Ponnen was secretary of the Durban branch of the National Union of Cigarette and Tobacco Workers; H. A. Naidoo held secretarial positions in the Natal Sugar Field Workers' Union and the Natal Sugar Workers' Union, and was vice-president in the Distributive Workers' Union. There were others: P. M. Harry, C. Amra, D. A. Seedat, R. D. Naicker, M. D. Naidoo, and A. K. M. Docrat.[4] A. C. Meer, one-time NIC vice-president, reflected in 1989 that in 1953 almost thirty of the NIC executive members held full-time offices in trade unions and community organisations.[5] Lakhani Chambers in Durban's Saville Street, the NIC headquarters, became the 'nerve centre' of the congress, trade unions, and youth organisations.[6]

Many of these individuals were affiliated to the SACP – H. A. Naidoo, for example, was the chairman of the Durban branch of the party – or made up the left-oriented blocs in the NIA or the NIC. They were prominent among the persons who inherited the leadership of the NIC in 1945. Others were part of the emergent middle class of professionals. In the way that the Indo-European Joint Councils provided a forum for the old leadership, so organisations such as the SACP, NEUF, and the Liberal Study Group (LSG) provided platforms for articulating newer strategies. The LSG bears close examination because it played an important role in shaping the policies followed by those who took over the reins of the NIC in 1945.

The LSG was established sometime after 1939. It met periodically to debate issues of the day. It was very active in 1941 and 1942, organising debates on topics of contemporary interest such as capitalism, imperialism, Zionism, and African self-government. It sometimes hosted a debate between two political figures, on one occasion between Yusuf Dadoo and S. M. Nana. Discussions occasionally centred on books of current interest.[7] I. C. Meer, who was at one time chairman of the LSG, argued that the organisation played a vital role in determining the leadership's position on key issues. Thus, for example, the LSG started a debate on the state-created Asiatic Affairs Advisory Board in 1943, and had helped the community as a whole to reach some kind of consensus on communal representation three years later.[8] The LSG gave rise to offshoot bodies such as the Women's Liberal Group and the Durban and District Women's League.[9] The LSG, and bodies like it, became intellectual forums for producing anti-communal and non-racialistic sentiments.[10]

Before looking at some individuals who became the new officials of the NIC, an analysis of NIC officials between 1938 and 1961 shows the following. Of the fifty-nine persons on the list for whom information could be found, thirty-seven had enjoyed some official position in the NIC before 1944. Their names do not appear after 1945, but they do appear in organisations, such as the NIO, which were set up in opposition to the NIC. Many of the thirty-seven had business connections. At least six of them were also members of the Indo-European Joint Councils. The balance show professional backgrounds: more than six attorneys, at least two physicians, and many who were connected to trade unions and real-estate business. Two individuals, Gopalal Hurbans and Vincent Lawrence served in important capacities before and after 1945.

Many of the leaders who assumed control of the NIC, and the TIC too for that matter, reflected the interests of Indians who felt neglected: an emergent middle class of professionals and civil servants; others who worked in retail and manufacturing establishments; and a growing segment of those employed in industries who might appropriately be called working class. The old leaders did address the needs of these sections of the Indian people. Indeed, their rhetoric often included references to the poor classes of Indians. But they were seen as part of a self-perpetuating élite concerned with their own commercial and business interests to the exclusion of those of the ordinary Indians; and their expressions of concern for others lacked conviction. Their failure to halt segregation might have been forgiven, but their willingness to barter away the rights of Indians called into question their sincerity – were they perhaps engaged in horse-trading at the expense of others for their own benefit? The new leaders exploited this disillusionment among the rank and file to their own advantage.

Who were the new leaders? What kind of new perspectives did they bring to the organisations they led? The profiles of some of the most prominent individuals are given below.

Dr G.M. (Monty) Naicker was born in South Africa in 1910. Not much is known about his grandfather except that he came to South Africa as a non-indentured immigrant; and his father, born in South Africa, established himself as a successful farmer growing bananas for local and foreign markets. Monty's father was wealthy enough to send his son abroad for education. But equally he was broadminded for a generation that feared sending sons far from home into an environment that was considered permissive. Monty Naicker left for Edinburgh and Dublin when he was seventeen years old, and there he completed the matriculation examination and a medical degree. These were important formative years.

Monty Naicker returned to Durban in November 1934 and established a medical practice. Soon after his arrival, a reception was organised for him by CBSIA and NIC. He was warned by one of the speakers to keep away from politics because they did not mix well with medicine. The Old Boys' Association also gave him a reception.[11] As a medical practitioner with overseas training, he obviously enjoyed some status, and local organisations sought him out as a guest speaker. He was invited, for example, to host a bazaar organised by the Hindu Youth Club on 16 December 1935.[12] Earlier, he presided over a session organised by the Clairwood Social and Debating Society.[13] Little else is known about the next six years until, in 1940, he joined the NIC. He was certainly active in the Liberal Study Group, which attracted professionals like himself to discuss political issues of the day. Naicker is listed as one of the members of the Nationalist Bloc in the NIA, which means that he must have been a member of the NIA at some point. What was it that propelled this young man to prominence in South African politics?

He may have been attracted to Marxist philosophy, which he no doubt encountered in his trade union activities, and in his association with members of the CPSA. As far as I know, he was not a member of the CPSA. He was, more accurately, a passionate Gandhi-ite. In an article Naicker wrote in September 1948, entitled 'What I owe to Mahatma Gandhi', his great admiration for Gandhi is quite apparent. He wrote that he began to appreciate the 'full power of the weapon of satyagraha' as he got deeper into Gandhi's writings. He re-read *My Experiments with Truth* in 1946 when he was in the Pietermaritzburg jail. It was not lost upon him that thirty-three years earlier, the same prison walls had held his great hero, and the man responsible for imprisoning him, namely Smuts, had also imprisoned Gandhi. Gandhi had made a pair of sandals to present as a gift to his captor.

When he and Dadoo flew to India to meet Gandhi, the sense of joy and excitement in Monty was overwhelming. 'Never before was my soul so wrapt in joy', he wrote. 'We were in the presence of a king of men, and in an instant we felt the glamour of royalty in the house', Monty remembered. Meeting Gandhi was an unforgettable moment in his life. He wrote, 'We will never forget the warm smile which lighted upon both of us – the smile of the hero we had loved and admired for thirty years.'[14] It is clear that Monty's idealism, his vision of the South African society beyond race and ethnicity, and his passion for service – and with it the sense of sacrifice – were all inspired by Gandhism. I don't believe he was simply a politician in a pragmatist mould: although he operated to some extent on this level, he was driven mainly by Gandhian ideals.

Seen in those terms, Monty's role in NIC and SAIC politics

becomes understandable. Monty accepted the challenge of leading the NIC after the conservatives had been ousted: he challenged the white power structure during the passive resistance campaign of 1946–48; he moved the NIC and also the SAIC into the congressional alliance with the ANC, when it became clear to him that the Indians could not by themselves defeat segregation and apartheid; and he subscribed to the multiracial vision of the Freedom Charter. Throughout all this he endured with courage his personal sacrifices: imprisonment during passive resistance, bannings throughout the 1950s, and the endurance of a long treason trial after 1956. Indeed, the bannings on Naicker continued until 1973. Monty, of course, was not alone in suffering from such repression, or in bearing it with such stoic valour. He surprised some of his contemporaries, who did not believe he had the will to sustain himself in politics. But two of them, I.C. Meer and Hassen Mall, thought very highly of him. 'His total opposition to apartheid', wrote Meer, 'had made him one of the most significant South African leaders respected by all engaged in the struggle of freedom.'[15]

Some said that Monty's speeches were drafted by others, and this may have been the case. But this question does raise the issue of whether Monty relied on others heavily for advice, and if so, whether he was subject to manipulation, especially by the communists. In an era that produced strong men in the liberation movement, this is entirely possible but I have not seen evidence of it. Whatever the truth, there were others in the NIC who were as dedicated as Monty Naicker.

There was H.A. Naidoo (1915–1971) who entered politics at the age of fifteen, and was among the individuals who made up the post-1945 NIC leadership. Naidoo, like several other top NIC members, was also a member of the CPSA serving on that organisation's central committee between 1943 and 1951. He was very active in organising African and Indian workers into trade unions, and was instrumental in improving wages in about twenty of Natal's major industries. He was popular among African and Indian workers. Naidoo and Sorabjee Rustomjee were deputed by the SAIC in 1946 to advise the

*The New Leaders*

Indian delegation to the United Nations on South Africa's Indians. Naidoo left South Africa in 1951 for the United Kingdom and there joined the British Communist Party, and even visited Hungary in the mid-1950s, but ceased political activities after 1955 because of disillusionment.[16]

N.T. Naicker, born in 1924, was one of the backroom boys who engineered the 1945 takeover of NIC leadership. He was a strong supporter of Monty Naicker. An attorney by profession, he held executive positions in the NIC and SAIC. At one time he served as the NIC's general secretary. In 1956, he was among the 156 individuals facing charges of high treason, but they were withdrawn in 1958. He was detained in 1960 in the state of emergency; and was also served with banning orders in the 1970s.[17]

Born in 1920, Marimuthu Pragalathan Naicker had a long and active career in politics both in South Africa and in exile. He was active from the beginning in the ousting of the Kajee-Pather group, and played important organisational roles in the passive resistance and defiance campaigns, as well as in the Congress of People. Although a truck driver, Naicker had organisational skills that served him well in unionising sugar workers; and his writing talents were put to good use when he edited in 1950 the *Guardian* and *New Age*, and later in exile the ANC organ, *Sechaba*. He was one of the accused in the 1956 treason trial. In 1960 and 1963, he was detained by the state and, in 1964, he was placed under arrest in terms of the 90-day detention legislation. In exile, Naicker served as the ANC's publicity and information director in London.[18]

Like N.T. and M.P. Naicker, Debi Singh (1913–1970) was not only part of the group that helped Monty Naicker come to power, but was very active in the NIC: general secretary from 1948 to 1953, and vice-president in 1954. Singh helped Monty Naicker and Dadoo to gain control of the SAIC in 1948. In 1946, he served as the secretary of the passive resistance council; and he participated in the 1952 defiance campaign. He was one of the persons charged with high treason in 1956, and was served with banning orders up to the time of his death.

Singh was a school teacher before becoming a farmer. He was active in the LSG, and served as its chairman in 1943. His politics were left-oriented, and he was a member of the CPSA.[19]

Dawood Ahmed Seedat (b. 1916) was active in the NIC from 1939, and served as the organisation's secretary between 1953 and 1955. Seedat, a bookkeeper, served in 1942 as the national secretary of the Indian Distributive and Clerical Employees' Union. He was a member of the Nationalist Bloc which actively opposed South Africa's participation in the war during its early years, and was jailed for his anti-war activities. I am not sure whether he was a member of the CPSA.[20] A couple of other NIC stalwarts were Gopallal Hurbans (b. 1915), and V. Lawrence (1872–1965) who were active both before and after 1945 in leading capacities. Lawrence had been active since the 1900s, as we saw in chapter two. The young Lawrence served as a clerk for six years in M.K. Gandhi's office. The remarkable thing about Lawrence was that, in addition to politics, he participated in a very wide range of activities that included sports, social welfare, religion, and education. He was a founder member of the Catholic Young Men's Society (f. 1895) and served as its president for eighteen years. He was a member of the Indo-European Joint Council, and served as its vice-president at one time. Lawrence was also a member of the Durban Consultative Committee of the Institute of Race Relations.[21] Both Hurbans and Lawrence strongly supported the new politics of the NIC, but neither was a member of the CPSA.

There were younger NIC members whose roles in the 1940s and 1950s were important in shaping the organisation's direction. J.N. Singh (1920–1996) and I.C. Meer (b. 1918) were both law students at the University of the Witwatersrand (Wits) in the mid-1940s and strongly supported passive resistance and the congressional alliance. They counted as 'radical' students, and used their legal and editorial skills to promote the liberation movement. They were contemporaries of Nelson Mandela, who was also a student at Wits, and the

NIC/ANC alliance is at least in part attributable to the vision they articulated. Singh and Meer were also members of the CPSA. Meer served as black student body president at the Natal University College in 1942. He was also active in the LSG, and was its president in 1942. Among the other positions he held was that of secretary to the Natal Teachers' Union. And his talents were fully utilised when he was given the task of editing the *Passive Resister*. Later, in 1955–56, Meer immersed himself in trade union work through SACTU, becoming the president of the Natal branch of this organisation in 1955. It is not clear whether Singh and Meer continued their membership of the Communist Party after it went underground in 1950; but they continued to play important roles in the NIC and the SAIC. As bright, energetic young men they certainly exerted great influence. Indeed, Jordan Ngubane considered Singh a popular hero in the 1950s. Whether or not any of their activities translated into 'control' of Indian politics, they certainly influenced Monty Naicker strongly.[22] Another young man who also played an important role was Hassen E. Mall (b. 1922), an attorney with a sharp intellect. He was a student in Cape Town at the time of the passive resistance campaign (1946–48), and supported it by establishing, with his friends, the Cape Indian Assembly to bypass the Cape Indian Congress which had refused to support the struggle. He served as one of the joint secretaries of the Assembly in 1950. Mall was also active in the India League which had been founded by C. Amra to promote India's independence. He was to play an active role in the NIC and the SAIC in the 1950s.[23]

Among the leading women of the time was Dr K. Goonam, who like Monty Naicker had trained as a doctor in Edinburgh and returned to Durban in the 1930s. She was quickly drawn into Natal's politics. Dr Goonam joined NEUF and participated in the LSG. She was soon to become involved in the Women's Liberal Group, and raised gender issues in a male-dominated NIC. Dr Goonam was to be one of the most active members of the NIC executive after 1945.[24]

Beyond Natal, there were individuals whose politics bore

close resemblance to those of many of the persons above, and whose roles in the TIC had a direct bearing on the NIC through their common affiliation with the SAIC. The three persons whose profiles appear below are Nana Sita (1898–1969), Yusuf Dadoo (1909–1983), and Ahmed Mahomed Kathrada (b. 1929).

Nana Sita was a staunch Gandhi-ite who continued to wear the white 'Gandhi' cap until his death in December 1969. Sita was born in India in 1898, and came to South Africa with his family in 1913. The Sita family owned and lived in a house-and-shop complex in Hercules near Pretoria, where Gandhi spent some time. He became active in TIC/SAIC politics in the late 1920s, and in the 1940s was among the individuals who identified with the new leadership. He took a leading part in the organisation of the passive resistance campaign in 1946, and himself spent a month in jail. Sita was the president of the TIC the year the 1952 defiance campaign was launched, and served on the joint planning council of the SAIC and ANC. He received a nine-month suspended sentence for his participation. Later, Sita was banned in terms of the Suppression of Communism Act although he was never a member of the CPSA. During the 1960 state of emergency, he was detained for three months.[25]

Although Sita had ceased to be politically active by 1960, he continued to oppose the Group Areas Act as its provisions threatened him with eviction from the premises the Sita family had owned since 1923. In an eighteen-page memorandum he submitted to the Pretoria magistrate's court on 7 August 1967, he called the law 'cruel, callous, grotesque, abominable, unjust, vicious, degrading, and humiliating to the utmost'. Indeed, he regarded the law as a 'crime against humanity, and a sin against God', for which the perpetrators would one day be judged. When Sita died in 1969, he was buried on the site from which he had refused to move.[26]

Dadoo represented in the Transvaal what Monty Naicker represented in Natal. He took over the leadership of the TIC from the old guard in 1945, and in the next three years was able to take control of the SAIC as well. In 1948, and again in 1952, he was elected to the presidency of the SAIC. Dadoo and Monty Naicker together shaped the course of South African politics. The two men had much in common, but there was also much that separated them.

Dadoo was born in Krugersdorp on 5 September 1909 into a business family. Yusuf was one of several children. After attending school in Krugersdorp and in Newton, a suburb of Johannesburg, Dadoo was sent to Aligarh College in India where he matriculated in 1927. Thereafter, he studied to become a doctor in Edinburgh and Glasgow, and returned to South Africa with impressive qualifications: LRCP, LRCS (Edin.), LRFP and S (Glas.). He established a medical practice in Johannesburg. He was soon to become involved in politics. Already he had shown a penchant for direct, militant action. In 1929, for example, he had demonstrated against the Simon Commission on its return to London from India, suggesting that he had carried over his anti-colonial stance from his days in India. Dadoo was to continue his fight against imperialism in South Africa.

It was clear that Dadoo believed passionately in the causes he espoused. There was nothing half-hearted about his actions and he showed great dedication. By 1939, the course of his political activism was clear: blacks must unite to challenge white supremacy, and the CPSA must guide the country to socialism. In 1937, he became a founding member of the NEUF. Two years later he joined the CPSA, and he continued to be a life-long member of this organisation both helping to organise it underground as the SACP, and externally while he lived in exile in London.

In 1938, he argued that the TIC should respond with passive resistance to a Transvaal law that sought to restrict Indians to segregated areas. Thugs hired by Indian conservatives almost killed him, but it was Gandhi's advice that dissuaded him from pursuing his own call for passive resistance. Dadoo helped to found the Transvaal Indian Nationalist Youth Organisation in June 1940, and as its first president he called the Second

World War 'a magnificent bluff perpetrated by the Imperialists . . .' Here he was using the CPSA line, and hoped to rally all blacks to oppose South Africa's participation in the war because, as he said, supporting the war would not bring them freedom. Dadoo was charged in January 1941 for his anti-war statements and was jailed for four months. When the Soviet Union became involved in the war, Dadoo had to make an about turn, and was assigned the task by the CPSA of finding intellectual justification for the switch in positions. After June 1941, the CPSA called for fair and equal treatment of black soldiers.

While Dadoo was to become more directly involved in Indian politics through his presidency of the TIC in 1945, and of the SAIC in 1948 and 1952 – and he thus played significant roles in the passive resistance and defiance campaigns – his arena of political activism was always non-racial and national in scope. For example, he became involved in the national anti-pass campaign in May 1944 as vice-chairman of the movement; and in 1946 he organised support for the striking mineworkers. He believed strongly that Indians had to ally themselves with the Africans, otherwise, as he said in October 1949 after his return from abroad, they had 'no justifiable grounds for survival in South Africa . . .' His role in the Indian congresses' alliance with the ANC must be seen as crucially important. Throughout he remained loyal to the CPSA, and when this organisation disbanded, to the SACP. Whatever hidden motives this may have involved, non-communist organisations welcomed his support and leadership. A singular honour was bestowed on him when he was awarded the Isitwalandwe Prize in 1955 by the Congress of People. Father Trevor Huddleston and Albert J. Luthuli were the other two persons who received this award.

There have been allegations that Dadoo, like other communists, sought to take control of the Indian and African congresses, and conspiratorial motives have been attributed to his activities. But the communists' ideological loyalties were known to all; and the non-communist organisations were only

## The New Leaders

too pleased to use their leadership talents on their platforms. Three of his contemporaries with whom I spoke, namely Meer, Mall, and Kathrada, all stated that Dadoo's passion for liberation was more important to them than his SACP affiliation. A young Kathrada saw in Dadoo a sincere, warm-hearted, and dedicated individual with charisma.[27] When, for example, Dadoo left South Africa in 1960, he was asked by the SAIC to officially represent this organisation abroad. Now that communist countries have opened their archives, one hopes to learn more about communist aspirations in the South African liberation movement of the 1940s and 1950s.[28]

When Ahmed Mahomed Kathrada, 'Kathy' to his friends, came to Johannesburg in 1938 from the outlying Transvaal town of Schweizer-Reneke, his intention was to complete his high school studies and move on to university education. He was sixteen years old in 1946 when he got swept into politics thanks to the influence of Dadoo and Moulvi Cachalia, a leading TIC member. In that year he helped to found the Transvaal Indian Youth Volunteer Corps, which would later become the Transvaal Indian Youth Congress (TIYC), whose purpose was to help in the passive resistance campaign. Indeed, Kathy became an active member of the passive resistance council, and was jailed for a month in December 1946 for his activities. This was the beginning of a political career that was to see him rise in the National Executive Committee of the ANC, and eventually occupy a position in the cabinet of South Africa's first non-racial government.

Like many others in the liberation movement, Kathy was a member of the CPSA and the congresses. A trip in 1951, while he was a student at Wits, took him to the Congress of the International Union of Students in Warsaw, and the World Federation of Democratic Youth in Budapest, where he spent nine months. Upon his return, he threw himself into the defiance campaign, which activity earned him a nine months' suspended sentence. He served in various capacities in the Indian congresses; and like many of his contemporaries, his freedom was restricted even further by banning orders. In

1956, he was on the list of individuals who were accused of high treason. Although politics was his primary concern, he was always interested in promoting education. For example, he helped to found in 1955 the ANC-run Central Indian High School in Johannesburg as an alternative model to apartheid education. Kathrada served as a full-time secretary of the school's parent body, the function of which was to raise money for the school.

After the banning of political organisations like the ANC in 1960, Kathrada continued to be part of the liberation struggle. In 1963, when he was arrested and convicted in the Rivonia trial, it became apparent that he was part of the ANC high command that directed the movement underground. The talents of this energetic thirty-five-year-old would be lost to the struggle – as indeed were those of others like Nelson Mandela who were convicted at the same time – for twenty-seven years. Kathrada was released from jail in 1989.[29]

In assessing the overall nature of the new leadership, it must be allowed that the overseas experience of people like Monty Naicker and Dadoo was important in shaping their perspectives. As students, they worked in a friendly and fairly open environment that enhanced their self-worth. Their academic achievements boosted their confidence. They were no doubt exposed to the burning social and political issues of the day, and may well have participated in the discourse on these on the university campus. Dadoo's student days were activist-oriented.[30] When these individuals returned to South Africa, they brought a broadened vision of a society free from racial prejudice and discrimination. An overseas professional training brought them prestige and social status. Both their own aspirations and the expectations others had of them propelled them into leadership positions. As physicians, their contact with people in need certainly enhanced their reputations.

Others in the profession who were important leaders were attorneys. This too was a high-prestige profession, thanks to its association with Gandhi, the attorney who had played an important role in South African Indian politics. We have seen how people like J.N. Singh and I.C. Meer were active in politics from their student days. They, like others who were not professionals but active in trade union work, were influenced by the ferment of the Second World War. The war's stated objective of promoting the liberation of subjugated people had raised their expectations. They drew attention to the contradictions inherent in colonial empires and the racial system in South Africa.

It was in this climate that the new leaders sought to play down race and ethnicity, and to promote a multi-racial congressional alliance. It was a kind of broad-frontism that ignored the ideological orientations of the supporters of the alliance. As a consequence, communists came to play an important role in the congresses. For people such as Hassen Mall, the ideological affiliation of people in the movement was of little consequence. What was important was their commitment to the cause of freedom. In 1946, some members of the NIC executive were identified as being communists. They were: M.D. Naidoo, G. Ponnen, Debi Singh, M.P. Naicker, R.D. Naidoo, Ahmed E. Patel, V.S.M. Pillai, A.K.M. Docrat, Billy Peters, N.K. Percy, and N.G. Moodley. An anonymous document, drafted probably in 1956, stated that thirteen of the forty-five NIC executive members were communists, and that NIC and SAIC conferences tended to take a pro-Soviet line in adopting peace resolutions. The document found the youth congresses to be more left-oriented than their senior counterparts, but otherwise found that communist influence in the Indian congresses was not dominant.[31] This is a question that needs further exploration. The nature and extent of communist influence may well suggest a more thoroughgoing impact on the liberation movement than has hitherto been acknowledged. Merely identifying communists in not enough, because a clear distinction must be made between a zealot like Dadoo and others who were lukewarm to the ideology even as declared communists. In any event, the role of the CPSA and SACP in the 1940s and 1950s must be placed within the context of the 'broader processes of transformation' in the

*Gandhi's Legacy*

ANC, and, I would add, the Indian congresses, as the editors of *Apartheid's Genesis* argue.[32]

This question should not obscure the fact, however, that most of the NIC leaders were dedicated individuals who were lacking neither in courage nor in their vision of the kind of society they wanted to create. All the people I spoke to about the leadership of this period, remember the executive members as being talented and dedicated individuals. They operated as a close-knit group. Even if Monty Naicker was influenced by strong individuals whose politics were left-of-centre, he was effective as a leader in keeping the group together. If there were squabbles in the inner circle – and apparently there was one between Naicker and M.D. Naidoo in 1956 or 1957 – they did not seriously undermine the operation of the NIC or deflect it from its main purpose.[33]

## Pioneer Presidents

Abdulla (or Abdoolla) Hadji Adam, the first president of the NIC

Sarojini Naidu, a well-known poet and Indian nationalist, who served as SAIC president between 1924 and 1929.

Albert Christopher was active in the NIC and SAIC in the 1920s and 1930s, and supported Gandhi in the satyagraha campaign. He broke away from the SAIC to form the CBSIA in 1933.

## Early Stalwarts

Vincent Lawrence (1872-1965) seen here with Archbishop Denis Hurley and Mrs Lawrence. One of the longest-serving members of the NIC, Lawrence engaged in a wide range of political and other activities.

## Journeyers against Injustice

Members of the SAIC deputation to India in 1925.
*Left to right: Standing* - Bhawani Dayal, V. S. C. Pather, S. Rustomjee, A. A. Mirza Galibbeg
*Seated* - J. W. Godfrey, Amod Bayat, Dr Abdulla Abdurahman

# Division and Unity

The NIA deputation to Prime Minister J. C. Smuts in 1943 is seen here with the High Commissioner of India. The NIA and NIC amalgamated soon after this.

## Passing the Baton

A. I. Kajee played a dominant role in Indian politics in the 1930s and 1940s. His leadership of the NIC was successfully challenged by the militants in 1945.

Dr Y. M. Dadoo assumed leadership of the TIC in 1945 and worked together with Monty Naicker to shape Indian politics in the 1940s and 1950s.

# Leadership in Troubled Times

*Top, l to r:*
G. M. Naicker
G. Singh
M. D. Naidoo

*Middle:*
A. I. Meer
M. Parekh
M. E. H. Ismail

*Bottom:*
N. T. Naiker
K. Moonsamy

# Defiance ... and its Price

Seen at an NIC conference are from left to right:
I. C. Meer, M. P. Naicker, Hassen Mall, G. Hurbans, J. N. Singh, S. M. Mayet, Debi Singh, and a Mr Patel from Johannesburg.

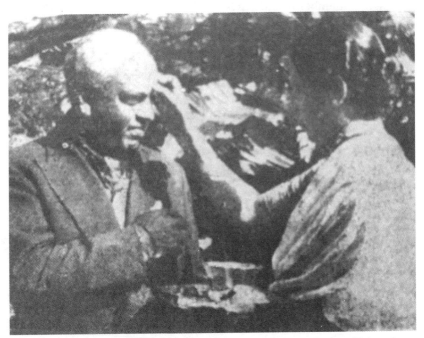

Mrs Naicker bidding farewell to Monty Naicker in the traditional Indian manner on his departure for Pretoria to face charges of treason.

## Links with the ANC and SACP

J. N. Singh, a member of the SACP, was a
popular hero in the 1950s.

Billy Nair joined the armed wing of the ANC
Umkhonto we Sizwe.

ANC Secretary-General Walter Sisulu, addressing an NIC meeting in Durban.

A. J. Luthuli, President-General of the ANC, is guest of honour at an NIC meeting. He is flanked by J. N. Singh on his right and Monty Naicker on his left.

## Onward to Freedom

Congress members canvassing support for COP.

A UDF rally in the Durban City Hall, 1970s.

## CHAPTER 5

# Broadening the Front

## 1940s and 1950s

> The day would come when there will not be a need
> for separate political organisations for the different
> sections of the oppressed.
>                     Monty Naicker, February 1953

The passive resistance campaign of 1946–48 and the congressional alliance of the 1950s defined the change in orientation of the NIC. The passive resistance campaign was an almost entirely Indian affair, but it nevertheless foreshadowed the multi-racial front of the 1950s. If the Indian congresses in Natal and the Transvaal had depended on the international climate to move the Smuts government to greater openness, they had sadly miscalculated the underflow of currents in white politics. Smuts's support had been eroded, and the 1948 elections returned the National Party which boldly proclaimed its intentions of implementing a stricter form of segregation under the apartheid system. The need for a more broadly based opposition was quite apparent to the congressional leadership. As a voteless minority making up no more than 2 per cent of the population, they could not hope to make much of an impression on a white political structure determined to hold on to power. It was an astute reading of the situation, and the Indian congresses attempted to strengthen their position by moving into organisational alliances with other bodies. They were not ready yet to merge with other organisations, as Monty Naicker's observation quoted above indicates.

This chapter examines the passive resistance campaign and the congressional alliance and the extent to which the first set the scene for the second.

**Passive Resistance**

The land issue and the laws relating to it were the specific instances around which passive resistance was organised. When the Pegging Act of 1943 expired, the Smuts government passed the Asiatic Land Tenure and Indian Representation Act of 1946. This law combined the provisions of the earlier law with an offer to Indians of indirect representation in parliament and the provincial legislature. Smuts was offering the Indians limited political rights in return for acceptance of segregation.

The NIC under Monty Naicker's leadership had already indicated its rejection of the bill before it was passed. A deputation had met Smuts on 9 November 1945, and when that produced no positive result, the NIC organised a mass meeting at Curries Fountain to proclaim 20 February 1946 as a 'hartal', that is a day of protest, pledge, and prayer with a cessation of normal work activities. An emergency meeting on 30 March 1946 declared the NIC's intention of launching a passive resistance campaign if the law were passed. A Passive Resistance Council (PRC) of twenty-five members was created to prepare for the campaign. The PRC met on 6 May 1946, publicly to announce the steps it would take to oppose the proposed law.[1]

The NIC action received support from groups in other provinces. The TIC under Dadoo's presidency elected a fifteen-member PRC at a mass meeting of seven thousand people. J.N. Singh, a Natalian then a student at the University of the Witwatersrand, was appointed secretary. The Natal and Transvaal PRCs were combined to form one Joint-PRC of ten members, five from each of the two provinces with Monty Naicker and Dadoo serving alternately as president. In the

*Broadening the Front*

Cape, the much smaller CIC was under the control of Ahmed Ismail who refused to support passive resistance. Indians who supported the movement in the Cape Province, however, formed three separate PRCs, one each for Cape Town, Port Elizabeth, and East London.[2]

On 2 June, the land and representation law was passed. The Indians' reference to it as the 'Ghetto Act' showed how strongly they felt about the law. June 13 was declared a 'hartal.' On that day, fifteen thousand Indians gathered at the Red Square in Durban and solemnly pledged to oppose the law. From there, a procession of passive resisters, led by Monty Naicker, marched to the corner of Gale Street and Umbilo Road where five tents were erected on a vacant municipal lot. There the first eighteen passive resisters took their stand.[3]

Eight days were to pass before the passive resisters were arrested on 21 July. They were found guilty but discharged with a caution. They went back to the tents to continue their defiance, and were arrested a second time. The resisters were released after being given suspended sentences. The next time around, the resisters were given jail sentences. Monty Naicker was the first to go to jail. On 27 June he was sentenced to six months' imprisonment. Sorabjee Rustomjee, M.D. Naidoo, Dr K. Goonam, and R.A. Pillay were also jailed. From the beginning of July, the courts decided to impose fines instead of jail sentences, with a threat to attach properties if they were not paid. None of the resisters paid the fines, and in a few cases their properties were sold at auction and the fines deducted. The amount fixed for first offenders was £3. Thereafter, the sentence was one month in jail with hard labour.[4]

By August, over 300 persons had gone to jail. Returning prisoners were given a warm welcome at mass meetings. Durban had supplied 37 batches of resisters by the end of September. The number of resisters from this port city amounted to 724, of whom 82 were women. Clairwood, Mere-bank, Wentworth, Isipingo, Seaview, Bellair, Dannhauser, Tongaat, Stanger, Ladysmith and Pietermaritzburg were some of the other places from which the resisters came. Beyond Natal's borders, individuals came from Johannesburg, Pretoria, Cape Town, Port Elizabeth, East London, and Kimberley. One batch came from Lesotho as well. Whites like the Revd Michael Scott and Mary Barr joined the campaign. Others like Mabel Palmer, E. R. Cussons, and M. B. Lavoipierre gave their support. They were among the white liberals who helped through organisations such as the Council of Human Rights and the Council for Asiatic Rights.

A second front was launched by the organisers on 19 August 1946. George Singh and four others occupied a vacant lot in Wentworth. But the authorities took no action and the camp was abandoned after two months. In September, Rugunath Singh, together with George Singh and his companions, occupied Rugunath's own house in the controlled section of Wentworth, but again no formal action was taken against them. There is no further reference to specific details about the course of the campaign in the 1947 agenda book, or subsequent minutes. It is therefore hard to follow the progress of the campaign in Natal.[5]

In the Transvaal, the TIC launched a passive resistance campaign on 13 June. A list of resisters issued by the TIC's PRC showed that 254 individuals, of whom 69 were women, had participated in Natal. Although figures are not available, there were also volunteers from the Cape.

On the first anniversary of the campaign, there was a mass meeting at the Red Square where certificates of honour were publicly given to those who had served jail sentences. Many were asked to relate their experiences.[6] The campaign was resumed in October 1947, but the government changed its tactics and declined to arrest the resisters. The NIC and the TIC resolved, however, to continue the struggle at mass meetings held in Durban and Johannesburg.[7]

A dramatic moment was reached early in 1948. The organisers expanded the scope of the campaign by targeting the 1913 Immigration Regulation Act, which prohibited, among other things, the interprovincial movement of Natal Indians to the Transvaal. On 25 January 1948, a batch of fifteen Natal resisters crossed the Natal-Transvaal border at Volksrust. Monty Naicker and Dadoo advanced from their respective borders. They shook hands as they met at a large road sign that marked the exact boundary point between the two provinces. After a ceremony that included speeches, the resisters proceeded to Johannesburg. On 26 January the resisters presented themselves at the Immigration Office for prosecution.[8] On 10 February 1948, Dadoo and Naicker were sentenced to six months' imprisonment for violating the 1913 law. Seventy-two persons were arrested at Volksrust; and twenty more were charged with crossing the border illegally. Among the persons leading batches of resisters was Manilal M. Gandhi. He did so on three separate occasions, and in violating the law he and the other resisters hoped to be arrested. The authorities, however, denied Gandhi the publicity his arrest would have brought. All the resisters except Gandhi were apprehended. Gandhi was allowed to go free on all three occasions.[9]

The organisers felt it was essential to disseminate accurate information through their own organs of communication. There were news bulletins like *Flash*, and *Weekly News Bulletin*; and *The Passive Resister* was a Johannesburg-based monthly newspaper that covered events under the editorship of I.C. Meer, then a student at Wits University. Pamphlet literature also appeared periodically, amongst which were included: *Five Months of Struggle*, *Resist the Ghetto Act*, *We Shall Resist*, and *How We Live: An Album of Photographs Showing the Living Conditions of Indian People in South Africa*. Much of this literature was aimed at the resisters themselves as well as at their supporters. There was also an overseas audience that the organisers hoped to reach. They hoped especially to canvass sympathetic nations at the United Nations Organisation in New York, and particularly India. Various individuals were sent to help India's Vijaylakshmi Pandit who presented the South African Indian case to the UN. They certainly succeeded in undermining the delegation sent out by the Kajee-Pather group. Dadoo and Naicker themselves

## Broadening the Front

*Racial breakdown*

| | |
|---|---|
| Indians | 1 638 |
| Coloureds | 48 |
| Africans | 16 |
| Whites | 8 |

*Age distribution*

| | |
|---|---|
| Between 18 and 30 | 1 476 (86%) |
| Between 20 and 25 | 1 175 (69%) |

The occupational backgrounds of 1 744 individuals are given in the report. Grouping them into related categories, the picture that emerges is as follows:

| | |
|---|---|
| Service-related workers | 604 |
| Labourers in factories, etc. | 529 |
| Housewives | 233 |
| Business owners | 183 |
| Farmers | 84 |
| Professionals | 52 |
| Students | 42 |
| Fishermen | 9 |
| Sailors | 8 |

If one combines the first two categories, those who predominated, that is 1 133 (65%), came from the lower to middle classes. The leadership in the movement probably did not reflect proportionately the classes that made most of the sacrifices. But the NIC's membership as a whole appears to be reflective of the above statistics. The total Indian population of Natal was around 200 000, and the NIC claimed to have a membership of 35 000, of which 2 per cent became directly involved in the campaign. If one adds volunteers and passive supporters, it is conceivable that as many as 20 per cent of its members supported the campaign in one form or another. This is not unreasonable in view of the fact that a crowd estimated at 15 000 gathered at the Red Square on 13 June 1946.

How did the whites generally react to the campaign? On the whole, their response was one of hostility. Even a liberal like J.D. Rheinallt Jones of the South African Institute of Race Relations did not approve of passive resistance as a method of defiance because, as he wrote privately, it introduced 'elements of force – and passive resistance is a form of violence – which must destroy hopes of democratic rule in the end'. The white press gave the campaign unfavourable publicity if it gave any attention at all. It had developed a pattern of anti-Indian reporting, and it saw no virtue in presenting the Indian case sympathetically. So a white backlash developed. In the first weeks squads of white thugs terrorised and even assaulted the passive resisters. Krishensamy Pillay was to die as a result of a savage assault. In February 1947, Natal's whites emphatically rejected the idea of giving the Indians even a limited form of municipal representation on a communal roll. Only 37 per cent (16 705) voted in the referendum, but of these 90 per cent said no. Vigilante forces in rural Transvaal towns mobilised a boycott movement against Indian traders. The movement spread to include Afrikaner agricultural, cultural and political organisations. Two boycott conferences were held: the first in Vereeniging in March 1947, and the second in Pretoria in April 1947. Afrikaner traders saw in the movement an opportunity to eliminate Indian competition.[11]

The newly-elected Nationalist government took a hard line against the leaders of passive resistance. It flatly turned down the NIC's request for a meeting. Minister of the Interior, T.E. Donges, speaking for the government, said he was not prepared to meet with an organisation that was 'communistic in [its] orientation', flouted the country's laws, and called for outside help. While the government had not then a clearly formulated policy on Indians, it was not going to follow the line adopted by the previous administration. Thus, it withdrew the communal franchise offered under the Asiatic Land Tenure and Indian Representation Act, and tightened the land tenure section. The family allowance for Indians was withdrawn, and racial restrictions in the Liquor Act were introduced. The government regarded the Indians as 'foreign and outlandish' – a part of the population that could not be assimilated – and spoke loosely of implementing repatriation schemes to send Indians to India. As late as 1951, the National Party government was pushing for repatriation, and doubled the bonus payable to individuals who wished to return to India.[12]

These developments deepened cleavages in Indian politics. Conservative groups had created alternative organisations: NIO (f.April – May 1947), TIO, SAIO (f.September 1948). They rejected confrontational approaches; and their willingness to consult with the authorities was welcomed by the government. Indeed, the government considered them 'acceptable channels', as Donges put it in his letter of 7 June 1948. An SAIO delegation was granted an interview on 26 November 1948.[13] A pattern for the future was established: the Nationalist government would use the conservatives to undermine the Indian congresses.

In assessing the significance of the passive resistance campaign, two points are important. The first is that it represented the culmination of the challenge to what the new leadership called 'appeasement'. The new leaders believed that Indians had every right to aspire to full equality. They were to discover how tenacious white supremacy really was. In specific terms, the organisers of passive resistance could count few instances of success. They did, however, discredit an accommodationist approach, and henceforth those organisations that advocated such an approach would be seen as aiding and abetting apartheid.

The second point is that the campaign marked the prelude to a strategy that was to unfold during the next two years. Passive resistance had shown a way to challenge white domination. Addressing the decision to disband the Native Representative Council, a Joint-PRC resolution of 25 November 1946 saw the significance of the campaign in a wider context:

We are of the opinion that the Passive Resistance struggle of the Indian people in South Africa is only a prelude to bigger and greater struggles and feel confident that the decision of the Native Representative Council will hasten the day when the alignment and unification of all non-European forces against oppression will become a reality.[14]

**Congressional Alliance**
The idea of a broad alliance of black organisations had been under consideration since the late 1920s. The Non-European United Front (NEUF, f.1927) addressed the issue without much success, as was discussed in chapter three. This objective was adoptped by the Non-European Unity Movement (NEUM, f.1943), an organisation that had a Marxist orientation. The Indian congressional leadership at the time was much too narrowly focused to consider alternative strategies; and after 1945 the new NIC leaders were gravitating to a non-ideological multiracial approach and could not seriously entertain the idea of joining NEUM's initiative.

The NIC-TIC leadership was open to the possibility of a black alliance during the passive resistance campaign. It gravitated to the ANC because the historical moment defining the need for alliance had arrived. All three organisations had leaders who had travelled abroad for their professional training and education, and whose broadened vision helped considerably in revitalising the politics in the bodies they headed. The idea of an alliance came from the Indian congresses. The minutes of the ANC's working committee meeting of 9 January 1947 refer to a letter received from the PRC about 'non-European unity'. The issue was raised in two subsequent working committee meetings, and may well have been discussed at the ANC's NEC. A 13 February 1947 working committee meeting decided on 'final steps' to be discussed with the 'Indian national organisation'.[15] It is quite possible that a man like Dadoo, who had a strong following among Africans and who drew huge crowds of black supporters at rallies, played a significant role in the alliance between the ANC and the Indian congresses.

*Broadening the Front*

So it was that Naicker, Dadoo and the ANC's Dr Alfred Xuma entered into a pact on 9 March 1947, committing their organisations to mutual co-operation in the future. Ironically, the NIC's relationship with Natal's ANC under A. W. G. Champion had not been particularly good. In any event, when the Dadoo-Naicker group took control of the SAIC in 1948, the ground was essentially laid for expanding the scope of the pact nationally.

The 1949 Durban riots underscored the need to cement the relationship between the Indian congresses and the ANC because of the potential for further divisiveness. The conflict brought about the death of 123 individuals and a massive destruction of property. That the Indians should be the target of the uprising suggests a deep distrust of them among rank and file Africans. Much has been said about the way in which the white establishment fanned anti-Indian feelings, but there were underlying causes for the friction that needed to be addressed. The congresses moved quickly to respond to the crisis. They engaged in relief work, and made public appearances in trouble spots. The SAIC and the ANC issued a joint statement on 6 February 1949, in which the disturbances were blamed on institutionalised inequality and the preaching of 'racial hatred' and 'intolerance' in 'high places'. A co-ordinating council was created on 15 April, the function of which was to generate greater co-operation between Africans and Indians. Naicker called for a united democratic front at the 1949 annual NIC conference.[16]

The year 1950 saw the SAIC and ANC draw closer together. At a special conference on 7 May 1950, convened by the ANC, 26 June 1950 was declared as a day of protest. The organisations that supported this call were: the ANC, the ANC Youth league, the APO, the CPSA, and the SAIC.[17] In the NIC presidential address of 1950, Naicker's metaphorical use of the language reflected how potentially dangerous apartheid was. A fear-driven ideology, it would reduce all to 'perpetual bondage'. The 'cancer of racialism', he said, was destroying all that was 'healthy' in South Africa. He warned English-speaking white

Natalians that their support of the ideology would lead to their undoing. Then, to underscore the need for unity, he said that democracy was indivisible.[18] ANC officials were, from about this time, regularly invited to perform the ceremonial task of opening SAIC and NIC annual conferences.[19]

The congressional alliance having been launched, the 1950s saw close collaboration between the Indian congresses and the ANC. Here we explore major manifestations of this in the Defiance Campaign, the Congress of People movement, and the Freedom Charter.

The Defiance Campaign was to mark the first time that the Indian congresses formally joined hands with the ANC to resist white supremacy. The fierce succession of laws passed to promote apartheid – the Population Registration Act, the Group Areas Act, the Mixed Marriages Act, the Immorality Act, and the Suppression of Communism Act, to name a few – had created a greater sense of unity and purpose among the black organistions. As Dr S.M. Molema saw it in 1952, while one black group had been systematically deprived of its rights, the other black groups had 'looked on passively or even contentedly to see it submerged by the steadily advancing tide of white exploitation and domination, little realising that it was their turn next to be similarly submerged'. Blacks must unite because another 'evil era of piracy and oppression' had begun.[20]

On 29 July 1951, the ANC and SAIC executives met in Johannesburg and mooted the idea of a campaign to defy unjust laws. The laws that were targeted were: the Pass laws, the Stock Limitation Act, the Separate Voters Representation Act, the Suppression of Communism Act, the Bantu Authorities Act, and the Group Areas Act. The laws were carefully selected for their impact on all sectors of the black community. The Pass laws affected all Africans; the Group Areas legislation seriously affected Indians and Coloureds; the Separate Voters Representation Act had taken away the vote previously enjoyed by the Coloureds; the Stock Limitation Act required the culling of stock and seriously affected African cattle

## Broadening the Front

farmers; and the Suppression of Communism Act defined communism so broadly that even those political activists who were not affiliated to the CPSA, which had disbanded itself, had become its targets. A Joint Planning Council (JPC) was established, and its twelve-page document was signed on 29 July 1951 by the ANC, the SAIC, and the Cape-based Franchise Action Council. At a ceremony in Thaba Nchu on 8 November 1951, J.S. Moroka, J.B. Marks, and Walter Sisulu signed for the ANC, and Dadoo and Y. Cachalia signed for the SAIC.[21]

The JPC's plan was to write to the government to demand the repeal of the targeted laws. This it did on 29 February 1952. The government failed to respond and, as arranged if this should happen, the JPC launched the campaign on 6 April 1952, a significant date as it marked the arrival and settlement of whites three hundred years earlier. Mass demonstrations occurred on that day in all major urban centres. The organisers had planned to run the campaign in three stages: first, commencement during which selected trained persons were to break laws in Johannesburg, Cape Town, Bloemfontein, and Durban; second, expansion of the campaign on new fronts; and third, the co-ordination of the campaign countrywide. Local, regional, and provincial councils were to organise volunteers, and funds were to be raised from one million people by the end of 1952, each person contributing one shilling. The JPC programme was approved by the ANC conference held in Bloemfontein in December 1951, and the SAIC conference that met a month later in Johannesburg.[22]

The campaign did not proceed as planned for a variety of reasons, among them the lack of adequate preparation and repressive state action. A total of 8 080 individuals participated in it. It was the strongest in the eastern Cape, the traditionally powerful ANC region, as the following figures show: 5 719 eastern Cape, 423 western Cape, 1 411 Transvaal, 269 Natal, and 258 Orange Free State. In Durban, the headquarters of the NIC, the response was weak. Some 37 centres were involved. For the Indians, it was a re-enactment of the passive resistance campaign: mass rallies at the Red Square in Durban, press releases for local and overseas media, and the distribution of news sheets.

Many of the same individuals were involved. Apartheid laws and regulations were defied. Twenty-one resisters accompanied by four thousand supporters marched from Nicol Square in Durban to the Berea Road railway station. The ANC leader, Chief Albert Lutuli, addressed the rally. Monty Naicker and the ANC's P.H. Similane were among the individuals who violated the restrictions on using apartheid-regulated public facilities. Ashwin Choudree, a senior NIC vice-president who led another batch a few days later, courted arrest, and told the Durban Magistrate's Court on 14 September 1952, that his peaceful violation of the laws would force the people who made them to see the 'error of their ways'.[23]

While in many ways the 1952 campaign was a repetition of the 1946–48 movement, the difference was that the earlier enthusiasm was missing. The campaign was disappointing to the organisers in many ways, despite its success in raising the political consciousness of blacks in general. In an assessment that followed the campaign, the NIC blamed the failure on organisational difficulties. The volunteers, according to an eight-page document drafted in December 1952 by the NIC for internal discussion, had not been sufficiently prepared 'theoretically' for the campaign. The organisers had not quite understood what was implied in the implementation of the M-Plan. Naicker stressed, in a related document, the need to inculcate the spirit of discipline; and stated that only when resistance was properly informed by such discipline, would the people be ready to undertake 'suffering and sacrifice'. The resisters needed to be trained intellectually in a programme that also included service in the form of manual labour, Naicker maintained. In any event, the government was able to destabilise the resisters through disinformation and by fueling ethnic rivalries. When violence resulted in the killing of three whites, including a nun, the government enacted two draconian measures, the Public Safety Act and the Criminal

Laws Amendment Act, and cracked down on the leadership.[24]

If the defiance campaign did not live up to the expectations of its organisers, it nevertheless set the stage for future collaborative ventures between the ANC and the Indian congresses. The campaign launched them into a new strategy, and their destinies were linked from then on. The congressional alliance came firmly into place. From these beginnings was to develop the Congress of People (COP) movement whose most lasting contribution to the liberation struggle has been the Freedom Charter, a document that would act as a beacon to the alliance in the decades ahead. The charter best articulated the ideals and principles of the congressional alliance, and offered a very different vision to that of the racial 'pigmentocracy' of apartheid.

Between 1952 and 1955, the congressional alliance expanded to include the South African Coloured People's Organisation (SACPO), and the South African Congress of Democrats (SACOD). This broad congressional front came to be known as COP, with an insignia depicting a wheel with four spokes representing united action under the slogan 'Mayibuye Afrika'. COP laid the groundwork for a mass gathering to adopt a freedom document.

The mass meeting took place in Kliptown on 25 and 26 June 1955. The delegates numbered 2 844, of whom 2 264 came from the Transvaal, 300 from Natal, 230 from the eastern and western Cape, and 50 from the Orange Free State. Urban centres were over-represented at the expense of rural and reserve areas. At this gathering, the Freedom Charter was adopted, a document that articulated a multi-racial vision of South Africa and envisaged a state with a socialistic orientation. I have not been able to determine the extent of SAIC/NIC input in the drafting of the document. Billy Nair recalled that he took with him the sentiments of workers in Durban he had canvassed on the shop floor, and had the opportunity to present them when he spoke at the Kliptown conference. Hassen Mall remembered that there was enthusiatic support for the document generally among NIC members.

The NIC was substantially involved in the COP campaign in Natal. At the formal launch in Durban on 5 September 1954, the NIC contingent was made up of 58 delegates in relation to the ANC's 81. COP hoped to collect a million signatures by 26 June 1956, in support of the Freedom Charter. By this procedure COP had hoped to popularise the document at the grass roots level. A People's Forum was instituted to reach the rank and file supporters. However, a year later only 10 per cent of the targeted signatures had been collected. The problem apparently lay in COP's inability to show the people the connection between the long-term goals of the document and the day-to-day struggle of the people. Besides, the organisers' drive to win support for the charter had not been sufficiently energetic.[25]

The Indian congresses continued to support the alliance, and participated in demonstrations, consumer boycotts, strike actions, targeted campaigns, and the like. They sought to mobilise Indian support under one banner. 'Our distinct and independent role in the Congress Alliance', noted the 1959 NIC secretarial report, 'is to see to it that the Indian people are brought into ever increasing participation in the constantly widening struggle for a non-racial South Africa.'[26] On the whole, the leadership was clear about its objectives, but it did not quite succeed in recruiting support at the grass roots level. Indeed, in 1955, the NIC adopted a resolution introduced by K. Moonsamy and Hassen E. Mall to implement the M-Plan, which refers to a strategy to organise supporters into street and area committees.[27] It is doubtful whether the NIC was able to pursue such an objective, because its leaders were increasingly hamstrung by the state's restrictions on them. The top echelon of the Indian leadership was among the 156 persons charged with treason, and it was tied up trying to defend itself against the charges for the next five years. The same individuals also suffered from banning orders.[28]

The SAIC/NIC agenda books of the late 1950s reflect newer

concerns. Questions were being raised whether passive resistance by itself was an adequate strategy for black liberation. Its potential could only be realised if used in conjunction with demonstrations, strikes, civil disobedience, and the like.[29] Perhaps it is in line with this kind of thinking that the later agenda books reflect a sharper focus on organising workers into unions and incorporating them into the political movement. Even though the focus on the Group Areas Act continued, it was placed within a larger context of the way apartheid was affecting all black groups. Under different circumstances, the Indian congresses may well have succeeded in continuing to play a useful role in the alliance. But that was not to be.

After the Sharpeville massacre of 21 March 1960, the ANC, among other organisations, was banned by the government. The Indian congresses were not banned, but their leadership had been effectively crippled by individual banning. Without the ANC, the alliance was shattered. The NIC put on a brave front in 1961, but the absence of the ANC had destroyed its political sustainability. It called for a national convention to hammer out a new beginning.[30] But the National Party was too well entrenched – it had just introduced a new beginning for South Africa by making the country a republic – to heed the NIC call. That call was repeated in 1971 when the NIC was revived, and would be repeated annually thereafter. When white supremacy was finally overtaken by circumstances in the late 1980s, the NIC's idea would reverberate in a broader alliance of which the ANC also became a part.

The Indian participation in the passive resistance campaign of 1946–48, was substantial and even enthusiastic in the beginning. In contrast, the response to the congressional alliance was guarded. The alliance signalled a kind of multiracial vision as articulated in the Freedom Charter that left many Indians ambivalent. The Indian congressional leadership, by its own admission, failed to prepare the ground adequately among its constituents. The doubts about how multiracialism would impact upon them in their daily lives

## CHAPTER 6

# Routine Business

## 1920s to 1961

The NIC's office holders were not financially rewarded for their work. They merely used the platform the NIC provided to plead the case for Indians to white decision-makers, individuals who were elected by white voters and therefore felt no pressure to respond. If the white elected politicians felt no pressure from the voteless NIC constituents, they nevertheless reacted out of a sense of paternalistic obligation. Their attitude seemed to be, be nice to us and we will see what we can do. Indeed, this became part of the strategy by which they sought to manipulate and control politics in the NIC. So, the NIC officials could plead, petition, and even threaten demonstrations to white office holders, but they could exercise little leverage on people who had been mandated by white voters to maintain and preserve white supremacy.

The conservative elements in Indian politics, and those in charge of the NIC in the early 1940s, became victims of this strategy. They always feared incurring the wrath of the white power structure if they should be seen to be too demanding. The militant elements felt differently. But whether conservative or militant, all NIC office-bearers were forced to use the parameters defined by whites. There were differences in emphases between the old and the new leadership in the NIC – the post-1945 leadership followed up demands for Indian rights either with direct action or the threat of it – but the issues and the routine established to deal with them did not differ greatly. This chapter examines the way in which the NIC routinely represented its constituents.

*Gandhi's Legacy*

Holding an office in the NIC gave the Indian leader status in the community, and this gave him some leverage both inside and outside the community. In appearing to speak for the interests of the 'community', the Indian leaders enhanced and reaffirmed their claim to leadership. In the 1920s and 1930s, the Indian leaders in the NIC, as indeed in the TIC and SAIC, played the role of 'patrons', and to the extent that they had the 'community' interests defined and measured, they could claim some success. Under a system that denied them legitimate political offices, they could say that they were doing their best. Take, for example, the NIC's offer in 1936 to represent the interests of the Natal Indian Cane Growers' Association at the plenary conference where a sugar agreement was being hammered out. The association apparently decided not to take up the NIC offer; and when Indian sugar growers were left at a disadvantage on price and export quota, the NIC blamed the association. 'For this calamitous state of affairs,' said the NIC secretarial report, 'none other than the Natal Indian Cane Growers' Association can be blamed for its obstinate attitude.'[1]

The 'community' that benefited from this 'patron' style of leadership was changing. The merchants and professionals who had dominated the community and who were served by the NIC, were being replaced by newer elements. While it is always hard to generalise about who made up the rank-and-file NIC supporters, it is accurate to say that middle and lower classes of Indians were beginning to be important as followers. It would be true to say that the 'patron' style, however well it may have served older constituencies, failed to serve the needs of the newer elements. But more than anything else, its moderate politics failed to stem the tide of anti-Indian discriminatory laws in the late 1930s and early 1940s. White supremacy's greed knew no limits; and the old leadership stood exposed and naked in the shreds of its failed strategy.

Those who benefited from this unsuccessful strategy were both the cause and the consequence of the newer directions in Indian politics after 1945. They redefined the 'community' they wanted to serve from a broader base; and indeed, they were justified in claiming to speak for the middle and lower classes of Indians, and among them the blue-collar workers especially. This new constituency required newer approaches shaped by different perceptions of problems, issues, and solutions. The new leadership was less inclined to look to India, the 'motherland' for solutions, although, of course India's status as an independent nation was to be fully exploited to help the cause of South Africa's Indians at the United Nations. The South African white power structure had to be confronted to find a home-grown solution.

The Indian political leadership generally looked to the national legislature to curb the discriminatory tendencies among local authorities. This is true at least until 1948, when the newly elected National Party government, with its apartheid programme for the whole country, began to reinforce local trends. Besides, if the NIC leadership could secure some rights and privileges nationally, it would not have to dissipate its energies pursuing local battles on many fronts. From 1940 to 1948, when Smuts was in power, the Indian leadership believed that the prime minister was open to pressure because of his standing among Western nations, especially the wartime allies, of which South Africa was one. Thanks to Smuts, South Africa's role in the war effort was not insignificant; and Smuts himself had had a hand in formulating the principles embodied in the United Nations charter. The NIC leadership took advantage of Smuts's position internationally, and the contradiction inherent in his upholding of principles at the UNO which he denied in his treatment of blacks in South Africa. This strategy did have some effect. The South African Indian issue became known in international forums. But in the final analysis, Smuts, ever the shrewd politician, almost always yielded to local white pressure. In any event, the illusion of achieving greater protection nationally, rather than locally, disappeared with the appearance of the National Party government, whose apartheid policies complemented what the local authorities had sought to do over the years.

Before discussing the issues that the NIC took up, it is necessary to comment on styles of NIC leadership. The old leadership before 1945 acted in a spirit of compromise, and was ready to strike deals. The post-1945 leadership was much more assertive in presenting the Indian case as a matter of principle. Both kinds of leadership drafted petitions, submitted memoranda, wrote letters, sought interviews and in other ways articulated the Indian position. Sub-committee and secretarial reports appeared regularly in the agenda books in which NIC activities were reported. The difference, however, between the old and the new leadership was that the latter was prepared to take politics to the street and to forge alliances with other organisations. Under these circumstances, the strategy also defined the overall political orientation. The NIC objectives transcended ethnic boundaries. Yet, in spite of this, three things remained the same. One, the issues they covered were the same; two, the NIC confined itself mainly to Indian interests; and, three, the membership remained Indian.

The NIC agenda books in the 1950s show greater concern with trade union issues, and here ethnic boundaries became blurred. This was the reality of the workplace – Africans and Indian workers laboured side by side. Among the NIC leaders were many who themselves had working-class backgrounds, although the leadership as a whole was made up of middle-class professionals. Some NIC officials had been affiliated to the CPSA until it was disbanded in 1950. The NIC identified with the common man, and therefore the concern with working-class issues appeared natural.

The NIC kept a close watch on local, regional and national matters that affected Indians, and it is to these that we now turn. After a closer look at how the NIC functioned, a short section examines the wrangle that surrounded the NIC assets after 1916. Thereafter, the chapter focuses on the issues the NIC took up in the following areas: land, housing and civic amenities, education, health and social welfare, trade and business, and agriculture and labour.

*Routine Business*

## How the NIC Functioned

The NIC executive consisted of a president, ten vice-presidents, two joint secretaries (until 1947 when the office of a general secretary was introduced) two joint treasurers, and a committee which numbered thirty, until 1947 when it was pared down to eleven. In 1947–48, some innovations were made, and these became standard practice in the years that followed. An executive committee of eleven persons was elected annually, together with a secretariat consisting of nine members, although the numbers could vary. The 'secretariat', perhaps an earlier idea that was revived, consisted of the president, the general secretary, one of the two treasurers, and several members of the executive; and it served as the inner core of the NIC's decision-making body. In earlier years, the appointment or election of a chairperson of the committee – A.I. Kajee for 1943–44 and George Singh for 1946–47 – served as a link between the top executive and the general executive members. The office of a full-time provincial organiser also appeared in 1947–48.

The NIC operated through sub-committees and/or *ad hoc* committees, each with a chairperson. These committees gathered information and recommended actions to be taken by the secretariat. The 1948 agenda book, for example, listed the following sub-committees: Information; Health, Social Services and Civic Amenities; Finance; Organisation; Housing and Expropriations; Education; Commerce; Industries and Agriculture; Labour and Employment.[2] In the late 1940s, the NIC headquarters was located at 5 Lakhani Chambers, Saville Street, Durban. It was run by a full-time staff made up of a typist, a shorthand typist, and a clerk.

Annually, four work committee meetings were required by the constitution to which the various branches sent their delegates. The secretarial reports from 1949 to 1955 (with the exception of 1952–53) complained about poor attendance. The 1955 average was 55 delegates out of a potential total of 219 in 17 branches. The burden of responsibility fell on the provincial executive which met on an average eighteen times between annual conferences. Most executive members attended the meetings regularly. The 1951 agenda book gave an attendance roster. The three people who faithfully attended seventeen out of eighteen meetings were: I.C. Meer, Debi Singh, and J.N. Singh. In some years, the work of the sub-committees was graded. The 1950 agenda book praised two of the sub-committees that did good work, namely Education, and Housing and Amenities. The Finance sub-committee had not done its job well, and the Organising sub-committee had failed completely, said the secretary's report. The performance of sub-committees varied from year to year as their membership changed.

The secretariat met more frequently. During the years for which numbers are given (June 1948 to June 1949, and June 1949 to June 1950), the secretariat met 53 and 50 times respectively. But the work of the secretariat, as indeed of the entire executive, was being seriously undermined by the political bannings of individuals who served on them. Between February 1954 and March 1955 the following individuals, who, among others, made up the NIC's inner core were banned: Dr G.M. Naicker (president), Debi Singh (general secretary), P. Naicker (organising secretary), S.V. Reddy, C.I. Amra, I.C. Meer, and J.N. Singh. The bannings would continue after 1955.

The NIC's branches were an integral part of the parent body. In 1940 there were twelve, and a year later this number increased to thirteen with the addition of Howick.[3] The 1940 and 1941 agenda books list branch officials, none of whom served on the provincial executive. However liaison was maintained, it is clear that the provincial executive was heavily Durban-based. Every annual conference between 1938 and 1959 was held in Durban. It seems that branches were expected to carry out the wishes of the central executive, send delegates to annual conferences, and in other ways maintain contact with the parent body. The December 1946 new constitution acknowledged the federal nature of the organisation, and accepted the principle of decentralisation.

But as the number of branches increased, this became difficult. There were twenty-eight branches in 1948–49. And, almost yearly, the general secretary reported branches inactive through 'apathy' and 'indifference'. In 1948, three branches were reportedly inactive and another four needed reorganisation. On the other hand, the Pietermaritzburg, Clairwood, Bellair and Seaview branches were active. Fifty or more individuals could establish a branch, and the payment of twenty-one shillings' affiliation fee entitled it to send three delegates to the provincial conference. For every one hundred members or part thereof, the branch was guaranteed three delegates. At the 1949 conference, twenty-two of the twenty-eight branches were represented. The six that had no representation were: Port Shepstone, Stanger, Chaka's Kraal, Riverside, Dannhauser, and Umkomaas. Indeed, the first three were considered defunct and eliminated in 1950. In 1951, seventeen out of twenty-three were considered to be active; and in 1955, this number went down to fourteen. The NIC attempted to stabilise branch membership through decentralisation and amalgamation, but the falling off in membership was also attributable to internal division.

I had access to the minutes of two branches, namely Durban Central (one meeting on 19 August 1956), and Merebank (eleven meetings between 31 July 1955 and 26 July 1956). The meetings dealt with two categories of issues: those that related specifically to the branch area, and others that were of common concern such as collecting signatures for the Freedom Charter and making help available for the COP campaign. The Merebank branch dealt with issues that might normally have been taken up by a ratepayers' association: street lighting, conditions of roads, providing a bus shelter, and holding educational classes. If the Merebank branch reflects issues normally handled by all branches, then the NIC sought to build support among its constituents by giving attention to local issues.[4] Many of the NIC activists did indeed succeed to positions of leadership in local organisations after the NIC ceased to exist in 1961. When the NIC was revived in 1971, these organisations came under their control.

To attract more members, and in line with its concern for the poorer classes of Indians, the NIC required the payment of only one shilling annually. Anybody over the age of eighteen was entitled to membership. In April 1948, the NIC claimed a membership of 34 942 individuals, but it is doubtful whether an accurate count was kept from year to year. In 1951, the number of members was exactly the same as in 1948; and in 1954, it was rounded off to 35 000.

The ebb and flow of the branch activities, and indeed of membership, are linked to perceptions of the NIC's effectiveness as an organisation. Debi Singh, who served with distinction as general secretary for at least four terms, observed in his 1951 secretarial report that the 'inconsistency' and 'lack of active interest' among the branches stemmed from the central organisation's own 'uncertainty and inactivity' since 1949. There was wider support when the NIC was seen to be actively involved, as was the case during the passive resistance campaign between 1946 and 1948. Singh's remarks only confirm, however, that despite embracing the principle of decentralisation, the NIC remained a highly centralised organisation. Branches had grown accustomed to centralised leadership, especially during the passive resistance years, and were cautious about taking initiatives on their own.

Only four of the agenda books between 1938 and 1961 supplied financial statements of annual operating expenses. The operating amount was £1 338 for 1940–41, of which clerical costs made up the biggest expense. For all years, income came from individual donors; and what is striking is that the donors were rich merchants on the NIC's executive. Nearly £850, that is two-thirds of the operating amount, came from about a dozen businessmen, the largest amount of £200 coming from E. M. Paruk, the NIC president. The NIC's operating expenses ranged between £2 000 to £2 500 after 1945; and even though the merchant dominance had disappeared, the money continued to be raised through individual dona-

## Routine Business

tions. The NIC was, however, capable of launching collection drives for special occasions. The passive resistance campaign raised an incredible £36 613 of which £32 212 came from donations (many from overseas sources), and £3 613 from an organised 'freedom fair'. The NIC owned fixed property in 1951 valued at £14 700 but the income from this, if any, was not reflected in the statements provided.[5]

### NIC Assets

At the time that the NIC was founded, seven trustees were appointed, one of whom was M. K. Gandhi, whose function was to administer the organisation's properties. It is uncertain how many properties were acquired by the NIC in the 1890s. A 1938 report recorded four properties, all in Durban, at the following addresses: 95 Prince Edward Street, 80 May Street, 197 Umgeni Road, and 199 Umgeni Road. On 15 July 1915, Lazarus Gabriel and six others obtained an order from the Natal Supreme Court to interdict the NIC officials from administering NIC funds. The court appointed George Mackeurtan as receiver for the NIC properties until the dispute should be resolved. Mackeurtan died and, sometime after his death, the administration of the properties passed into the hands of a Durban law firm, Messrs Livingstone, Doull and Dumat.

After a period of time, the Master of the Supreme Court decided that the NIC had ceased to exist, and ordered all monies of the organisation to be deposited with him. The law firm of Messrs Livingstone, Doull and Dumat continued, however, to administer NIC funds. It was in response to the Master's decision that Gabriel and his six co-applicants formed a new Natal Indian Congress on 6 March 1921. The aims of the NIC remained the same. The old membership fee of sixty-three shillings per year was originally retained, but then scaled down first to ten and a half shillings, later to five shillings, and much later to two and a half shillings. The NIC's new executive allowed some years to pass before it made an application on 25 October 1925 for the court to set aside the order of 15 July 1915. However, the court denied the application on the grounds that the re-established NIC was a new body and had no legal claims to the assets of the original NIC.

Nevertheless, the organisation's executive registered the NIC in terms of the Companies Act of 1926, and defined its objective in terms of the law for legal purposes. The object of the 'company' in terms of the third clause of the act was to advance the interests of Natal's Indians, that is to improve the conditions of the Indian community in all spheres, and to foster good relations with 'various sections' and 'races' of South Africa. The NIC executive was to be made up of a president, ten vice-presidents, two joint secretaries, two joint treasurers, and thirty committee members. The central executive was to oversee the growth and establishment of local branches. Provision was also made for women's branches. Branches were required to pay 50 per cent of the membership fee, which was fixed at two and a half shillings per member annually.

The legal wrangle continued apparently up to the time that the law company submitted a report to the NIC's first conference in 1938.[6] The value of the Prince Edward Street property was placed at £2 680, and that of the other three combined at £1 670. The Guardian Fund balance stood at £2 755. In March 1950, the NIC appealed to the Supreme Court to transfer the Guardian Fund revenues to the NIC coffers, and the fixed properties to nine trustees it had appointed. The trustees, from the new leadership of the NIC, were: Dr G.M. Naicker, Dr B.T. Chetty, V. Lawrence, A.E. Shaikh, H.J. Randeria, A.I. Meer, M.M. Gandhi, Pasaw Seebran, and C.N. Rana. The application was opposed by P.R. Pather and C. Anglia, who were members of the former old guard of the NIC, which suggests that their decision to oppose was in part politically inspired.

By 1953, the court had decided to transfer the Guardian Fund and the properties to the NIC. The NIC created the Mahatma Gandhi Educational, Social Welfare, and Charitable Trust controlled by eleven trustees. The eleven trustees were

*Routine Business*

leading members of the NIC: Dr G. M. Naicker, V. Lawrence, Dr A. H. Sader, Dr B. T. Chetty, A. E. Shaik, J. N. Singh, I. C. Meer, S. M. Mayet, G. S. Naidu, A. Choudree, C. Hurbans, and Debi Singh. But this new trust had no organisational connection with the NIC. It seems that the leadership feared government confiscation of NIC assets. Some in the NIC opposed the move, imputing ulterior motives.[7]

## Land, Housing, and Civic Amenities

The attempts to place Indians into separate areas go back to the nineteenth century. Law 3 of 1885 in the Transvaal provided for separate trade and residential areas. The British protested, and so a year later it was amended to exclude separate areas for trade. Even after the British had achieved political hegemony in 1901, the efforts to segregate Indians into 'locations' and 'bazaars' continued. The British were not opposed to segregation, but were prepared to allow exceptions to be made in favour of the Indian élite. In Natal, the colonial legislature used the trade licence laws effectively to regulate the location of Indian traders. In the 1900s, only a handful of Indian traders remained in Durban's West Street, the main downtown thoroughfare of business. In the Transvaal, the 1908 Gold Law prevented Indians from acquiring land in mining areas; and the 1919 law further entrenched the principle of separate areas in the Transvaal.

In the 1920s, the Class Areas Bill and the Areas Reservation Bill were introduced in parliament with the intention of implementing nationally the policy of segregating Indians into separate areas. The campaign launched by the Indians against these measures was to result in the Cape Town Agreement of 1927 between the governments of India and South Africa. The agreement halted the move to segregate the Indians for a while. The South African government had hoped that the Indians would leave the country voluntarily under a state sponsored scheme. But this did not happen. By the late 1930s the issue of racially defined separation for Indians resurfaced. Laws passed in 1935 and 1939 tightened earlier provisions made in the Transvaal. In Durban, where the Indians made up one-third of the population, the issue of Indian 'penetration' of white areas flared up with a vengeance.

The Natal Municipal Association, reflecting white opinion, had raised the issue of Indian penetration into white areas, and wanted legislation to prohibit it. The Township Ordinances of 1924 and 1926 had made it possible for anti-Indian clauses to be introduced into leases and title-deeds; and in rural areas, the Unbeneficial Occupation of Farms Act of 1937 threatened to deprive Indian farmers of their land. White ratepayers' associations generally wanted segregation legislation to prevent Indians from expanding into areas they considered and defined as white.[8] The NIC denied these charges of penetration and accused whites of fear-mongering. It acknowledged the growth of the Indian population in Durban, the result of the steady drift that was occurring in the 1920s and 1930s from the rural areas. Indeed, by 1938 the Indian population in the city had trebled.

The charges of Indian penetration into white areas intensified around 1939 and continued throughout the war years. A series of state-appointed inquiry panels investigated the charges, and mainly dispelled them as pointed out in chapter three. The DCC was able to get the commission's terms of reference defined more narrowly to obtain the desired result. The DCC and NMA were interested in radial racial zoning. In Durban, some of the wealthier Indians had purchased properties in white areas for investment rather than residential purposes. The Indians themselves responded to these charges in a variety of forums. For example, the NIA submitted in 1941 a 180-page memorandum. It had carefully examined land acquired by Indians in all of Natal after 1927, and made out a solid case for the lack of foundation of the charges of penetration.

The memorandum dealt extensively with Durban. It made a blistering attack on the Durban City Corporation (DCC) not only for its racially motivated actions, but for failing to provide adequate housing for the growing Indian population in the city.

*Routine Business*

Around 1940, there were over 83 000 Indians, of whom over 59 000 lived in newly added areas such as Clairwood, Mayville, Cato Manor, Merebank, Overport, Clare Estate, Sydenham, Riverside, Springfield, Wentworth and Jacobs. These were mainly Indian areas which the Indians themselves had helped to develop. In the old Borough of Durban, where whites were three times as numerous, and whose properties were seven times more extensive, the situation had remained fairly static. The memorandum pointed out that whites had new areas to go to such as Stellawood and Morningside, and yet the DCC had expropriated areas that were predominantly Indian for white expansion. This was the case with Indian-owned lands in places like Merebank, Sydenham, and Riverside.[9]

In spite of Indian opinion, which was unanimous in rejecting segregation on principle, white pressure for legislative action continued. It resulted in the passage of the Pegging Act of 1943. The circumstances around the passage of that law, the Pretoria Agreement, the 1946 Asiatic Land Tenure and Representation Act, and the passive resistance campaign that was subsequently launched, have all been discussed earlier in this study. The NIC mounted a vigorous campaign of defiance.[10]

Whatever success the campaign enjoyed in popularising the Indian cause abroad, and awakening political consciousness among Indians in South Africa, it did not deter the newly elected National Party government. The new government scrapped that part of the Asiatic Land Tenure and Representation Act of 1946 that offered communal representation, and declared its intention of pursuing segregation under apartheid more vigorously. Neither the Indians, nor indeed the other blacks, realised at the beginning how severely the policy of apartheid was going to affect them. The war, and the climate of liberation it generated, had raised expectations among blacks generally. So when the laws of apartheid appeared, they dropped on them like bombs.

For the Indians, the Group Areas Act of 1950 embodied everything they had feared about residential segregation. It appeared to them that the Nationalist government aimed at destroying their livelihoods through forced removals and confiscation, and in that way compelling them to return to India. Indian repatriation was a long-established goal among the Afrikaner Nationalists. The NIC, and even rival organisations like the NIO and TIO, devoted enormous energy to resisting the Group Areas Act throughout the 1950s. The SAIC, under the control of new leadership by 1950, co-ordinated these initiatives nationally.

Local authorities such as the DCC had all along wanted segregation written into law, and they were entirely happy with the passage of the Group Areas Act. The law provided for racial zoning for business and residence: it was Law 3 of 1885 all over again, and more. The 1950 law involved confiscation of properties, and forced relocation, a kind of ethnic cleansing. For the Indians who, for example, held substantial vested interests in businesses and residences in the Grey Street complex of Durban, the Group Areas Act was an attack on the very lifeblood of their existence.

At the annual provincial conference of the NIC in September and October 1950, Naicker warned that the English-speaking Natalians who supported group areas were 'unconsciously bringing their own doom nearer', because democracy was 'indivisible'. Apartheid threatened everybody's liberties. Driven by fear, this ideology was making South Africa into a 'rigid, caste society', and was reducing the blacks to 'serfdom'. He repeated his warning the following year. Apartheid's laws drove home the point that democracy could not be divided into racial compartments, and inspired closer co-operation among black political organisations. Naicker repeatedly called for black unity, and the Group Areas Act served well to rally Indians, who were the most seriously affected by it, behind the idea. Indeed, it became one of the targeted laws of the 1952 defiance campaign.[11]

The NIC hoped to ready people to resist the Group Areas Act. Towards this end, it held meetings, drafted memoranda, and organised special conferences. The first of such memoranda was submitted by the NIC on 18 February 1953 to the Land Tenure Advisory Board with reference to Durban. The population in the city in 1951 was: 132 841 Africans, 16 104 coloureds, 145 744 Indians, and 131 430 whites. The memorandum pointed out that the DCC's housing and land policies had pushed Indians to the outskirts, further and further from the city's centre. Indians owned 10 000 acres of land with properties valued at £25.5 million compared to the nearly 16 500 acres held by whites whose property value was placed at over £113 million. But group areas threatened the Indians fundamentally, and its implementation would be devastating.[12] There were, no doubt, other forums through which the NIC kept the spotlight on the Group Areas Act.

When the law was proclaimed in 1956, the NIC gave attention to the question of its implementation with even more vigour. An inclusive Group Areas Conference was organised for 5 and 6 May 1956. It was attended by 191 delegates representing 68 different organisations. Thirteen branches of the NIC were represented.[13] Monty Naicker's paper at the conference pointed out that 157 016 were likely to be displaced by the law with a racial breakdown as follows: 81 886 Africans, 6 292 coloureds, 64 745 Indians, and 3 462 whites.[14] The conference established a vigilance committee whose task was to distribute literature on all facets of the law.

The *Government Gazette* of 6 June 1958, gave notice that the process of implementation of the Group Areas Act would begin in Pretoria and Durban. The NIC created a special vigilance committee for the Province of Natal. It organised a demonstration at Curries Fountain in Durban on 26 June 1958, which was attended by thousands of people. The NIC was in possession of statistics supplied by the Minister of the Interior in Parliament. The figures of people expected to be moved were: 750 000 Indians, 8 500 coloureds, and 1 000 whites. These figures would certainly have alarmed those present at the Curries Fountain rally.[15]

An NIC memorandum dated 2 October 1959, reviewed proposals for Durban, and described as 'blatantly discriminatory', the way in which they were going to affect the black residents. A total of 469 000 blacks faced removals, of whom 231 000 were Indians, and their property value alone came to £30 million. The proposals were 'immoral, iniquitous and unjust', and the NIC vowed to fight them 'tooth and nail'.[16] As more and more areas were proclaimed, the NIC offered a programme of legal advice to the ratepayers' associations within them, and also co-ordinated mass protest gatherings.[17]

The SAIC, of which the NIC was a constituent body, also took up the campaign against the Group Areas Act. Under control of the militant leadership of the NIC and the TIC, the SAIC went beyond its co-ordinating function to determine policies. And its most significant decision was taken in 1951 when it decided to join the ANC in launching the defiance campaign. The Group Areas Act was selected quite naturally as one of the laws to be targeted by the campaign.[18]

Even though the conservatives had parted company with the new leadership of the NIC and SAIC to form their own political bodies, they nevertheless were opposed to the Group Areas Act. They had proportionately more merchants and property-holders in their numbers, and so stood to be most adversely affected by the law. Writing for the SAIO, P.R. Pather produced a 42-page memorandum condemning the Group Areas Act.[19] The SAIO submitted in 1950 or 1951 a memorandum against the Group Areas Act.[20] In the end, the conservatives of the NIO, TIO, and SAIO took the position that since the state intended to implement the law regardless, they should secure the best possible advantages for Indians. For example, the memorandum submitted by A.M. Moola and P.R. Pather to the Group Areas Board in November 1961, argued that those areas in central Durban that had an historically 'unique Indian character' should be zoned for Indians. They were speaking of the Grey Street complex, and as members of the Central Durban Property Protection Committee they appeared to represent traders and property-owners mainly.[21]

Housing, slum clearance under the Slum Act of 1934, and civic amenities were issues that were closely related to the land question; and like the land question, they featured prominently at every NIC annual conference. The 1938 NIC conference urged the DCC not to displace Indians from areas considered to be slums in and around Durban, at least until alternative accommodation had been found. Parts of Bell Street and Warwick Avenue in Durban, and sections of Riverside and Jacobs were on the DCC's target list.[22]

The DCC's projected plan was to relocate displaced Indians to areas on the city's periphery. One such area was Cato Manor, which the DCC had purchased around 1925 for the purpose of erecting an Indian village. Cato Manor was then beyond the municipal boundary. By 1933, lots were being sold, and a scheme to build economic and subeconomic houses had been instituted to cater for the poorer classes of Indians. The NIC opposed from the very beginning the creation of Cato Manor, because it was discriminatory. There were areas within the borough to which the city could relocate displaced Indians.[23] The NIC continued to speak for individual landlords seeking to postpone the demolition of condemned buildings and, where appropriate, supported requests for housing loans for renovations.

Expropriation of Indian-owned land by the DCC was another issue on which the NIC took a strong stand. The NIC suspected, with good reason, that the DCC's objective was to introduce racial zoning by means of expropriations and evictions. The DCC's support of the 1946 land tenure law and the 1950 Group Areas Act confirmed the NIC's suspicions. After 1950, racial zoning became a national policy, and the DCC supported it fully. An ironical twist to all this occurred in 1950 when the DCC proposed to expropriate 300 acres of Indian land in Cato Manor to build houses for Africans. The NIC had opposed the creation of this area on principle, yet opposed the expropriation on the grounds that such an action took away land from people who had little enough. The Cato Manor Indian Ratepayers' Association joined the NIC in this opposition.[24]

The natural increase of the Indian population, which rose

from 107 000 in 1946 to 144 000 in 1951, added to the acute housing shortage. Suburbs like Sydenham, Merebank, Wentworth and Clairwood were seriously affected. Yet the DCC's social engineering, aimed at moving Indians away from the centre, and certainly away from the whites, continued. The idea of opening up white areas for Indians was never seriously entertained. Around 1955, for example, the DCC planned to build low-cost housing in Merebank so as to accommodate Clairwood Indian residents. The NIC objected on the grounds that Merebank would in the future be zoned for industrial development.[25] Despite such objections, and the NIC's strong representations to the Group Areas Board, the DCC went ahead with its planned development of Indian residential areas beyond the city's boundaries.

Towards the end of 1960, for example, the DCC secured a huge expanse of land to the south – and in the process displaced scores of Indian banana farmers – to house 50 000 to 60 000 Indians in what is today Chatsworth. A similar scheme was proposed along the northern coastal region around Verulam. The idea was to create a huge belt of Indian settlements around Durban's periphery. The DCC, said the NIC, was a 'great planner of Indian ghettos'. The expropriation involved in the resettlement of people was a 'great plunder,' and was 'grim[ly] reminiscent of the mass confiscation of property under Hitlerism . . .'[26] The NIC worked closely with ratepayer associations to educate Indians about the Group Areas Act, and leading NIC individuals, among them Hassen E. Mall and I.C. Meer, became involved. Since Indians had no political rights, the solutions offered were usually legal in nature.[27]

In addition to the NIC's focus upon expropriations and removals, it also annually raised the issue of the absence of proper civic amenities in Indian areas. Roads and drains were frequently in a state of disrepair; public swimming baths and other recreational facilities were either segregated or nonexistent for blacks; and public transport was not adequate besides being racially divided. Central public libraries were segregated or, where alternative facilities existed, they were inadequate. In a gesture of defiance, the NIC's J.N. Singh, Ashwin Choudree, and C. Amra entered the Durban Central municipal library in 1949 and 1950. They created a minor stir, but library segregation continued well into the 1970s.[28] In some areas, like Ladysmith and Pietermaritzburg, and indeed in Durban itself, Indians were allocated low-lying areas that periodically flooded during heavy rains. Curries Fountain, a sporting facility for whites was closed to Indians – and the alternative facilities provided at Springfield were poor. Apartheid on the beach front was a perennial bone of contention.[29]

## Education
Education was the issue that most consistently received attention in the NIC agenda books. The Indian school population increased dramatically in the 1940s and 1950s due mainly to the youthful age profile of the Indians. The greatest need was initially at the primary level, but as more and more of the pupils finished their first years of schooling, the pressure mounted for high school and even tertiary institutional accommodation. Between 1927 and 1936, the Indian school population increased by 250 per cent. The NIC focused on the threefold nature of the educational issue: the shortage of schools; the inadequate and discrimination-based allocation of resources; and segregation.

The 1949 NIC agenda book suggested that as many as 30 000 Indian children of school-going age had no access to schools. The 1957 agenda book listed statistics that more accurately reflect the numbers of children without place in the schools: 16 029 (1951), 13 145 (1953), 9 244 (1945), 8 882 (1955), 12 000 (1956), and 9 207 (1957).[30] If there was a steady improvement in the situation, it was only because the authorities alleviated the situation by employing the 'platoon' system, in which two or more sessions were run to accommodate the pupils using the same facilities. Nobody was happy with it, but it was accepted as a temporary measure.

In education more than in other areas, the Indian leaders showed greater co-operativeness in spite of ideological differences. On 18 April 1953, the NIO established the Indian Education Committee (IEC) to which the NIC not only gave support but with which it was prepared to work collaboratively. The IEC organised a private platoon system; and in other ways tapped the resources of Natal Indians to build schools with matching funds, or improve existing education facilities. In these endeavours, the IEC could call upon the expertise of Dr S. Cooppan, a leading educationist. The 1957 agenda book claimed that of the 83 000 Indian pupils in 1956, 78 per cent had been accommodated in schools built by the Indians themselves.[31] The IEC held conferences in the 1950s, and made representations to educational authorities on Indian education.[32]

The NIC itself was very active in education. In 1947, for example, the NIC education subcommittee met with various white public officials, including Prime Minister J.C. Smuts, to provide a first-hand report of Indian educational needs. One of the issues was the fact that only one institution, namely Sastri College, served the high school needs for all Indians in greater Durban. To make up for this inadequacy, the NIC established the Congress High School (CHS). The CHS opened its doors to over a hundred pupils on 16 February 1948, and was officially inaugurated by Monty Naicker a week later. In the first few weeks, volunteer teachers used the Kathiawad Hindu Samaj until, on 3 March, it was relocated to the Greyville Indian School. M.B. Naidoo, who was appointed the honorary principal, at one stage had twenty-five teachers under his authority. Students paid ten shillings in school fees which was doubled later, but reduced sometime thereafter when the state provided seven and a half shillings subsidy for every pupil. Fees obviously did not generate sufficient revenue to run the CHS, so NIC funds and private donations were used to make up the deficit.[33]

The teaching staff was paid five shillings, later seven and a half shillings and in 1955 eleven shillings, although I was unable to determine whether this was a daily, weekly, or monthly rate. The number of students varied: about 100 in

## Routine Business

1948, 140 in 1949, 400 in 1953, 200 in 1953–54, and about 40 in 1955–56. The 1948 budget for the school was £593, and this doubled to £1 185 in 1949. During 1953 and 1954 the operating expenses amounted to £702 and £821 respectively. The school helped to prepare pupils for the standard 8 public examination. Statistics for selected years show success: 45 passed in 1950, and 37 out of 58 passed the examination in 1953–54. There are no further references to the CHS in the agenda books after those of 1956.[34]

The NIC insisted on equality as a matter of principle, even if the schools were segregated racially. The disparity in the per capita expenditure between Indian and white pupils stood at a ratio of one to three. Indian teachers at public schools continued to receive lower salaries. The NIC, in consultation with the Natal Indian Teachers' Society, took up these issues with the authorities. The NIC often sought to confer with public officials, but did not always succeed in gaining access to them. The IEC was considered apolitical and had easier access to white public officials. For example, Dr G. Shepstone, the Natal provincial administrator, for some years refused to meet with NIC officials.[35]

The NIC pushed for access to institutions that would provide Indians with skills in the technical fields, teacher training, or special skills for disabled individuals. As for university education, the NIC was critical of the segregated parallel sessions run by the University of Natal; and it rejected the idea of a separate university for Indians when the Natal University College principal suggested it in 1947. The NIC's position did not change when the Nationalist government passed the 1959 Extension of University Education Act with the intention of creating a separate university for Indians. It attacked the creation of such 'tribal' institutions; and on 17 December 1960, organised a conference to pass a resolution on 'total non-cooperation' with the Salisbury Island College (later University of Durban-Westville) that was then being established. The institution's aim was 'to indoctrinate the minds of our students into accepting servitude'. The NIC looked into the possibility of providing Indian students with alternative facilities by which they could prepare for degrees through institutions in London.[36]

While the NIC was actively involved in promoting the educational welfare of Indians, it continued to believe that education should be non-racial and free from ideological bias. Thus it was critical of the government's proposed Christian National Education plan, calling it a 'Nazi plan', and speaking out against the Bantu Education system designed specifically for Africans. It was generally opposed to the principle of racial exclusion, and so whenever the opportunity arose, as for example in admitting Africans to the Indian-run M. L. Sultan Technical College, it took a firm stand. But, of course, segregation was becoming more deeply entrenched under apartheid; and regardless of its principled stand, the NIC simply had to work with ethnically and racially defined institutions among its constituents.

## Health and Social Welfare

The economic depression of the early 1930s affected all South Africans, and the NIC taddressed bread and butter issues affecting the Indians in Natal. Such issues included old age pensions, relief funds, free milk to children, grant-in-aid for indigent mothers, burial services for those who could not afford them, and other kinds of social services. During 1939–45, the NIC also focused on wartime profiteering by merchants.

After the war, the NIC was less concerned with taking up individual health and social welfare cases – although this continued to happen – and became more concerned with correcting the ills in the system. Discrimination and segregation deprived Indians of the full enjoyment of available health and social services. Thus, for example, the NIC continued to argue for equal access to state-run hospitals and clinics; it worked to end discrimination in public employment; and, to improve work opportunities for Indians, insisted that the ban on their moving from one province to another be lifted.

The NIC was quick to provide services to Indians in moments

of crisis. This was especially the case after the racial disturbances in January 1949. The NIC joined the NIO in organising
relief funds for the victims of the riots, but blamed the
disturbances on the 'differential and discriminatory treatment'
of blacks based on racially-skewed political, economic, and
social structures in South Africa. The animosities generated by
the riots had to be brought under control, and toward this end
a co-ordinating council of African and Indian leaders was
established on 15 April 1949.[37]

While the NIC continued to work for Indian interests in the
1950s, the congressional alliance required that it articulate
those interests in a broader context. Thus, the NIC supported
consumer boycotts, and did relief work for political detainees
and the treason trialists between 1956 and 1961. It generally
supported the idea that all should have access to public
institutions regardless of race, colour or creed.

**Trade and Business**
The NIC agenda books from 1938 to 1941 periodically referred
to licensing boards, and white municipal boards, which often
denied licences to Indian traders. In Natal, this was a long-
standing issue going back to the Dealers' Licences Act of 1897,
which sought to restrict Indian trade in Natal. The Rural
Dealers' Ordinance of 1923, the Borough Ordinance of 1924,
and the Township Ordinance of 1926 similarly attempted to
curtail Indian trade. In the 1920s and 1930s, trade restriction
was considered a serious issue, in part because the NIC
leadership was dominated by the merchant class. In and
around Durban, especially at the Indian market, and in the
rural areas of Natal, whites sought to use licensing (and shop
hours ordinances) as a means of eliminating competition from
Indians.[38]

The disabilities did not, of course, disappear in the 1940s and
1950s, but the NIC agenda books made fewer references to
them; and this in part reflected the non-merchant and even
anti-merchant character of the new leaders, who arranged
their priorities differently.

## Agriculture and Labour

There are numerous references to NIC intervention, in many cases relating to Indian sugar and banana farmers, as well as to industrial disputes involving Indian workers in the clothing, metal, and railway industries. The grievances of Indian tailors and meat retailers also received the NIC's attention. Other instances included the unfair token system in the coal-mining industry, workman's compensation and, in general, industrial legislation that was discriminatory.[39]

While the earlier NIC efforts were concentrated around Indian workers' rights in individual and specific instances, the post-1945 NIC was substantially concerned with workers' rights in general, reflecting the organisation's closer ties with the trade union movement and the working-class backgrounds of the NIC rank and file. Some of the NIC's leaders were communists, and no doubt wished to build up a worker constituency. The NIC supported SACTU, the umbrella organisation of non-racial trade unions, because it recognised its potential in the anti-apartheid movement.[40]

As onerous as it was for the NIC to perform its duties in routine matters through members who gave freely of their spare time, the state imposed restrictions on them and thus made their task even more difficult. The NIC's active leaders were banned individually, or listed as communists in terms of the 1950 Suppression of Communism Act. In either instance, they were prohibited from appearing on public platforms, delivering speeches, and in other ways carrying out their work as leaders. Key members were in this way prevented from taking actively prominent roles in the NIC. Debi Singh, for example, was an efficient general secretary whose banning from 1949 to 1953 meant that he had to cease performing his duties. Monty Naicker was banned in 1954, and every year following that, his presidential speech was read out at the NIC annual provincial conferences. He managed to run the NIC *in absentia*, but clearly missed the advantages of personal leadership.[41]

Many of the same individuals in the NIC leadership were

accused of high treason in 1956, and had to be present for the respective duration of their trials in Pretoria. If the state's intention was to tie up the leadership in this manner, it succeeded well because the treason trialists were unable to lead normal personal and professional lives, not to mention carrying out their usual political responsibilities. The NIC agenda books after 1956 reflect fewer activities of a routine nature.

While the state moved in this manner to immobilise the NIC officials, and thus to discredit them, it sought at the same time to promote moderate and conservative leadership. Thus the local white power structure preferred to work with the NIO or SAIO members; and at the national level, a similar trend was apparent. For example, the Durban city authorities ignored the NIC's A. I. Meer on the question of forcing Muslims in 1949 to use the municipal abattoir and chose instead to consult an NIO official.[42] At the national level, the government favoured the SAIO with an interview, and not the SAIC. The secretary to the Minister of the Interior, T. E. Donges, wrote to the SAIO on 23 July 1948 giving his reason:

> Your organisation being . . . neither communistic in their orientations or leadership, nor associated with any organised flouting of the laws of the country, and not looking to the political aid of another country while claiming to be composed of Union citizens, are regarded by the Minister as an acceptable channel through which the Indian population may approach the government for the discussion of any matter affecting its interests.[43]

Much the same position was taken by Prime Minister J. G. Strijdom in 1956.[44]

The state's divide and rule policy generally worked. The NIC and SAIC's lack of easy access to local and government officials made their task of representing Indians on specific matters more difficult. They were part of the congressional alliance and as such saw the representation of their case in a larger context.

## CHAPTER 7

# Revival and Resurgence

## 1971 to 1990

A crowd of twenty-five thousand congregated at a rally organised by the NIC in 1961. It proved, however, to be merely a
flare before the flame flickered and died. There are no records
to show the official activities of the NIC over the next ten
years, although its high-ranking members may well have met
informally from time to time. Many of the top NIC executive
members were under banning orders that severely restricted
their ability to run the organisation; others went into exile to
continue their political activities. A few like Billy Nair, George
Naicker, and Ebrahim Ismail joined the armed wing of the
ANC, the Umkhonto we Sizwe. Some of these details are given
in a book by Natoo Babenia, *Memoirs of a Saboteur* (1995). The
South African Indian Congress was expected to speak on
behalf of the Indians through exiled Yusuf Dadoo who was
given this responsibility. The absence of official activities for
the rest of the 1960s suggests that the leadership had been
totally unprepared for the crushing blow that the congressional alliance had suffered. A demoralised leadership withdrew. At the branch level, however, it is quite possible that the
members who were attending to local concerns may have
joined ratepayers' organisations, or established such bodies.
They probably re-emerged to play prominent roles when the
NIC was revived in the 1970s.

The Nationalist government was emboldened by the absence
of serious censure from its leading trading partners in the West
who continued to pour investment into the country. Indeed,
the early 1960s was a period of unprecedented economic

growth in South Africa. Having silenced black opposition groups and hearing no dissent from the West, the government proceeded to refine and develop apartheid into an implementable system. In terms of apartheid's broad objective, the Indians were to be separated from other blacks for the purpose of ethnically differentiated administration.

After accepting the principle that Indians were a permanent part of the country, the Nationalist government created in 1961 a Department of Indian Affairs. Twenty-one Indians were nominated to a body that was called the South African Indian Council (SAIC), an advisory organ that the government hoped would replace the South African Indian Congress which had virtually ceased to exist. The message was clear: the state was not prepared to accept any other body as a channel through which Indians could express their opinion, and used considerable patronage to give the SAIC credibility; and from time to time, its status and membership were revised. In 1968, for example, the SAIC became a statutory body, and its membership was increased to twenty-five. The body was enlarged to thirty in 1974, one-half of whom were henceforth to be elected indirectly through a system of electoral colleges.

The government's efforts to impose such an institution from above no doubt served in part to galvanise individuals into reviving the NIC. Since the late 1960s, blacks had been generally seeking to redefine their goals and strategies in the face of apartheid's continued onslaught. For instance, the Black Consciousness Movement (BCM) sought to prepare blacks culturally and psychologically to assume leadership and control of their own liberation. Students were in the forefront of the BCM at university campuses, and with time they would seek to make alliances with other groups.[1]

The decision to revive the NIC in 1971 came in the wake of fears that the SAIC, serving narrow business interests, had entered into a deal with the government over the future of Durban's Grey Street complex, in which the city's Indian businesses and residences were concentrated. Many saw SAIC members as willing to accommodate the government at the expense of the Indian masses in much the same way that conservative Indian politicians of the 1930s and 1940s had been. At a meeting on 25 June 1971 at Durban's Bolton Hall, an *ad hoc* committee was established under the chairmanship of Mewa Ramgobin, who had spearheaded the revival. Other members were: George Sewpersadh, Bill Reddy, Billy Naidoo, Paul Ramesar, D. Bundoo, B.D. Maharaj, M.R. Moodley, N.N. Naicker, and S.P. Pachy. The committee tested public opinion by visiting communities in many parts of Natal, especially the poorer ones. It wasn't only concerned with Indians. As Ramgobin put it, 'Politically for us it was important to show that we were concerned not just with Indians but African workers as well.'[2]

There was intense campaigning in the weeks following 25 June. Branches were established, and a working committee prepared for the NIC convention scheduled for 31 October 1971. Ramgobin, whose five-year banning order had been lifted in November 1970, was banned for a second five-year term in September 1971. He was thus prevented from participating in the convention, and thereby probably denied the NIC's first presidency after its revival. But the convention proceeded as scheduled at the Phoenix Settlement. The significance of the location was not lost on the organisers: the settlement had been established in 1904 by Gandhi, the man who had founded the NIC. Thus began a significant phase in the NIC's hundred-year journey.

The post-1971 leaders, in striking contrast to earlier leadership, were individuals with professional backgrounds. They were almost all well educated, and had an excellent command of the English language. A high percentage of them could claim descent from indentured or free Indian grandparents, which they could use occasionally to show that they were not part of an élite group with vested interests. George Sewpershad and M.J. Naidoo, who served as president for most of the 1970s and 1980s, were attorneys. R. Ramesar, who served as secretary, was a social worker. Ramgobin ran his own insurance agency in Verulam and had a novel to his credit.

Farouk Meer was a physician, and Fatima Meer and Jerry Coovadia were academics. It is probable that the branch officials, too, would have come from professional backgrounds.

## A Defining Moment: The First Decade, 1971–1981

An amended constitution was adopted in 1972. The amended document did not differ much in specific details from the earlier constitution. Clauses (a) to (d) under 'Objects' broadened the NIC's overall goals:[3]

(a) to strive for a united democratic South Africa on the basis of universal adult suffrage;
(b) to promote the cause of all the oppressed people of South Africa and to oppose racial discrimination;
(c) to promote peace, understanding, and goodwill among people of all races in South Africa;
(d) to co-operate with all organisations irrespective of race that are striving for democracy by non-violent methods.

A unitary, non-racial South Africa, based on universal suffrage, was the ultimate goal of the NIC. Yet its membership was confined to Indians resident in Natal, aged eighteen and over. Despite the NIC's non-racial orientation, the leadership retained 'Indian' in the organisation's name. Whereas the earlier enrolment form bound a member to abide by the rules of the NIC constitution, the new enrolment form left no doubt about the organisation's non-racial thrust. Signing members agreed to 'accept the principle of the Natal Indian Congress as set out in the Freedom Charter'.[4] It is clear that the old name was retained for historical reasons. There was much to be gained by leaving intact the Gandhian connection. The leadership may also have considered the logistical convenience of organising Indian activities in neighbourhoods that were segregated by race.

But the name issue continued to be a source of uneasiness and conflict. At the July 1973 annual NIC conference, the Pietermaritzburg branch proposed that the organisation's

*Revival and Resurgence*

name be changed to the 'South African People's Congress' since the NIC as a 'purely Indian' body was 'an anachronism'.[5] The meeting was unable to resolve the issue, and referred it to a ten-person subcommittee to explore 'the desirability' of establishing a non-racial organisation.[6] Nothing, however, came of its deliberations. When it reported back on 15 September 1974, it suggested that the NIC should convert itself into a 'united democratic front' type of organisation, but it was unable to determine what support this move would receive from other bodies.[7]

Inherent in the name issue was the question of the nature of the organisation, and this was to cause a dispute with the South African Students' Organisation (SASO). When the NIC was revived in October 1971, SASO warned that 'all forms of sectionalism' would hurt the black cause, and that the NIC should 'give effect to the movement of black consciousness and black solidarity . . .' The NIC rejected the SASO call at an executive meeting on the grounds that black consciousness promoted race exclusiveness which was an apartheid concept. NIC secretary, R. Ramesar, went even further and charged SASO with propagating the policies of the Pan Africanist Congress, banned in 1960. SASO denied the charges, and insisted that the NIC retract its statement or, at the very least, apologise for the false accusations. When the NIC refused to do this, SASO's Saths Cooper resigned in June 1972 from the NIC executive. SASO accused the organisation of having adopted a 'killer' approach towards it. Whether the NIC's reaction to SASO was a deliberate misrepresentation of the black consciousness philosophy or not, it is clear that the NIC leadership wished to maintain a separate identity for its organisation with its Gandhian connection and Indian membership.[8]

Organisational details are sketchy in the minutes of the annual conventions. The need for maintaining close links between the branches and the provincial executive was expressed in 1973. Branches needed a 'programme of activity'. The secretary reported increased branch activities in 1977–78, although no details are provided. The 1978 annual conference expected at least twenty branches to be represented, but no exact number is given, nor are the branches identified. In other organisational matters, there is reference to nine executive meetings in the 1977 report, but otherwise such details are missing.[9] The 1978 conference reported that two vacancies on the Gandhi Memorial Trust (f. 1960) had been filled. But details on the NIC's finances are absent from the reports.[10]

The NIC continued to express its unqualified support for a free society, and rarely missed an opportunity to point out that apartheid was antithetical to such a goal. It regularly engaged in symbolic gestures to heighten political awareness, and in that way to maintain a sustained mood of defiance. So, the 1960 Sharpeville massacre was commemorated; the independence of Angola and Mozambique in 1975 was celebrated for its likely impact on white rule in South Africa; and support was shown for the Soweto students who rose up in 1976. Individuals who were significant in the liberation movement were remembered: Rick Turner after he was assassinated, Braam Fischer on his death, and Steve Biko after his murder in police cells. The NIC mourned the loss of people who died in detention, among them H. Haffejee and B. Mzizi. And, of course, the banning and detention of its members were treated with considerable seriousness – their sacrifices should not be forgotten. People like Mewa Ramgobin, George Sewpershad, and Fatima Meer were remembered.

Beyond the symbolic gestures, however, the NIC hoped to link up with local organisations and thus build grass roots support. The NIC identified closely with students at the University of Durban-Westville, throughout the 1970s, in their battles with apartheid-supporting officials and teachers. The NIC executive sometimes intervened directly with the university authorities on behalf of the students, or backed parent-support groups that addressed student grievances. The NIC also supported industrial strikes that erupted in Natal in 1973, and in some instances brought the workers' complaints before the employers. The NIC actively took up the case of displaced stall owners in Durban's Victoria Street market, and of families left homeless by the floods in the Springfield area. The organisation sought to identify itself with the poorer classes of Indians, and nowhere was it more successful than in Phoenix and Chatsworth, two areas around Durban in which Indians were concentrated. The NIC became involved in such issues as housing needs and high rents. The rent increases of March 1980 led the NIC to establish the Durban Housing Action Committee (DHAC), a body representing twenty organisations from seven areas in and around Durban. DHAC organised a women's march on the City Hall, and forced the Durban City Council at least to call for a rent moratorium.

The NIC often co-ordinated its activities with groups and organisations that shared its goals. On a number of occasions the NIC shared a platform with the Labour Party whose leader, Sonny Leon, remained defiantly opposed to apartheid's structures. It also associated with the Citizens' Action Committee and Natal University's Wages Commission looking into wage and salary disparities. The NIC worked closely with bodies that promoted non-racial sports to discourage people from participating in apartheid sports events. People like Hassan Howa and Morgan Naidoo, who organised non-racial sports, were applauded. And in 1976–77, the NIC appeared to be making an attempt to heal its breach with the black consciousness organisations about the time they were outlawed.[11]

In its drive to challenge and discredit political structures created by the government, the NIC worried about the state's possible success in co-opting a growing middle class of Indians that enjoyed material benefits in suburban areas like Umhlatuzana, Reservoir Hills, Westville, Durban North, and La Mercy. The establishment of the SAIC and local affairs committees had created openings that offered lucrative rewards. The NIC's fears were that materially satisfied elements among the Indian population would become complacent and weak in resolve. This dilemma sparked off a debate in the NIC's inner circle of leadership: should the organisation fight apartheid from within by accepting positions in government-created structures as the Labour Party had done, or should it continue to reject these institutions totally. The Labour Party leader, Sonny Leon, had opted to fight apartheid from within, but the government had simply co-opted others to get around the obstacles. In the end, those in the NIC who argued for continuing the struggle from the outside prevailed. That apartheid's creations constituted mere 'window dressing democracy', not real democracy, and should therefore be denied credibility and legitimacy, was the prevailing view.

When, therefore, a decision was taken in 1979 to make the SAIC fully elective, the NIC launched a campaign for its total rejection by the Indians. An anti-SAIC committee was formed in May 1979, and in October an anti-SAIC convention was held to which, no doubt, individuals from the Transvaal and the Cape Province also came. The government was uncertain what the Indian response would be in the first national SAIC election, and kept postponing the election date. It tried various devices, including compulsory voter registration, to ensure a good turnout. Finally, it selected 4 November 1981 as the date of the SAIC election, by which time some 297 040 Indians out of a total of 350 000 eligible voters had registered.[12]

Meanwhile, the anti-SAIC campaign gathered momentum. The NIC's efforts were combined with those of organisations in the Transvaal and the Cape. In the Transvaal, an anti-SAIC committee representing 150 organisations had been formed under the leadership of Dr Essop Jassat.[13] On 10 and 11 October, weeks before the elections were scheduled, another anti-SAIC convention was held at which 110 organisations were represented, among them the NIC. The convention produced a Charter of Change with a preamble which read:[14]

> We South African democrats, gathered in Durban on this day, recognising the unequivocal rejection of Government-created ethnic institutions by the oppressed people and having experienced this directly in the Anti-South African Indian Council Charter of Change, declare for all South Africans and the world to know that the

*Revival and Resurgence*

struggles of the past 25 years have convinced us that the only viable alternative to the present exploitative and repressive system is one based on the principles for meaningful changes, politically.

The NIC and its allies used every possible forum to campaign against the SAIC elections. At well-attended public meetings, a whole range of well-known speakers used their oratorical abilities to argue against the SAIC; individuals spoke to smaller, well-targeted groups; meetings were held in the homes of people; students engaged in door-to-door campaigning with leaflets; articles appeared in newspapers, but mainly the anti-SAIC message was spread through paid, full-page advertisements in newspapers. The anti-SAIC forces were fortunate to have the services of school children, whose widespread dissatisfaction with the educational system had resulted in a boycott movement in 1980–81. The message of the anti-SAIC campaigners was simple enough: the SAIC was a useless body serving apartheid, and those who were prepared to serve on it were doing so for nobody's benefit but their own. Dr Jassat said, '. . . we refuse to give the SAIC our mandate because we see separate political institutions as fundamental to the apartheid system. And we refuse to submit to the indignity of approving the instrument of our own oppression.'[15]

The anti-SAIC forces were highly successful in their stated goal of keeping the Indian voters away from the polling booths. Nationally, only 10.5 per cent of the registered voters cast their votes. In some places like Fordsburg in Johannesburg, the percentage poll was as low as 1.75 per cent. Rural areas generally registered higher percentages. The anti-SAIC campaigners, among them the NIC, could claim victory. The government had certainly suffered a setback. But the government was not to be deterred, and proceeded to build credibility in the SAIC around vested interests. Unrepresentative though it may have been, the SAIC was the only body, recognised by the apartheid regime, through which decisions on Indians would be made.

**Striking Out With the UDF, 1981–1990**

Having created elective bodies for the coloureds and Indians, apartheid's ideologues considered moving white supremacy a step further. Pressure had been building up in the 1970s for some kind of reform at least, to show that the government was moving away from domination. Since the policy of creating homelands envisaged a long-term solution for the African majority, a plan to accommodate the coloureds and Indians, who in 1980 made up 9 per cent and 2.9 per cent of the population respectively, was necessary.

The idea of co-opting these two minorities into a three-parliament system, with the white minority making up the third, was introduced in 1977. With the help of people like Samuel Huntington, a conservative professor of political science at Harvard, the regime refined and improved the concept.[16] Based on the principle of segmenting political authority ethnically and racially, Pretoria hoped to create three separate units within one political system. Africans would have no share in the system as they would belong to the homelands system. Each of the three minority groups would have authority over its own affairs as was then the case administratively. But in areas of common concern, as in defence, the economy, and foreign relations, the control would be jointly exercised with a strong presidential form of leadership at the helm.

A President's Council was appointed in September 1980, and was given the responsibility of devising a new system under terms of reference strictly defined by the government. It produced a document that largely corresponded with the government's own plan of a three-parliament system. The document's most salient features were then incorporated into a draft new constitution. The state president ratified the new constitution on 22 September 1983. The constitution was approved by a margin of 66 per cent in a referendum of white voters only. The government feared rejection by coloured and Indian voters, and so their opinions were not tested.

The new constitution provided for a tricameral parliament,

one chamber each for whites, coloureds, and Indians with a ratio of 4:2:1, which in actual numbers would amount to 178, 80 and 40 members. All decisions from the three chambers would move to the President's Council, a nominated body consisting of 41 whites, 13 Coloureds, and 6 Indians. Leaders of the majority parties in the chambers were promised ministerial portfolios in the government's cabinet. This, then, was the structure under which coloured and Indian voters were asked to go to the polls on 22 and 28 August 1984.

The NIC had rejected the three-parliament idea in principle as early as 1978 when M.J. Naidoo said in his presidential address that it was 'nothing short of total prostitution of [the] democratic process'.[17] Some years later when more details of the government's constitutional plan became known, the NIC reconfirmed its rejection. In 1982 or 1983 a twelve-page NIC memorandum argued that the dominant white ratios at all levels indicated that the government had no serious intention of creating a non-racial South Africa. The apartheid edifice remained in place, it argued, and could not be negotiated out of existence within the newly proposed system. The memorandum called for all 'patriotic forces' to join hands in launching a 'united democratic front'.[18]

A later memorandum spelled out the objections to the proposed new constitution in greater detail. Its importance lies, however, in its articulation of an alternate vision of South Africa based on the Freedom Charter, and in advancing theories on why and how the new constitutional dispensation 'imposed from the arrogant heights of apartheid', should be derailed. The memorandum feared that the Indian middle class might find 'consociational democracy', as envisaged, attractive. 'If the middle class is compromised,' the documenter said, 'there are possibilities that they can drag in a significant portion of the Indian South Africans with them and thereby put our struggle for a non-racial democracy many years back.' The NIC's role was clear: expose apartheid especially to those who would likely be 'seduced', and persuade them that their 'security and destiny' lay in 'national liberation and not [in] ethnic expediency'. The NIC's clarion call was to build strong, democratic, community-based organisations around workers, women, and the youth, especially students.[19]

The NIC, then, was among the organisations calling for a broadly united and co-ordinated opposition to the proposed new constitutional plan. The call was made officially on 23 January 1983, by Allan Boesak, who had just become the president of the World Alliance of Reformed Churches, at the Transvaal Anti-SAIC Conference. Each province created a co-ordinating committee. In Natal, the NIC leaders served on the committee. Boesak's appeal was to lead directly to the creation of the United Democratic Front (UDF) later in the year. The launch of the UDF occurred on 20 August 1983 at Mitchell's Plain in Cape Town. At this meeting, some 575 organisations were represented, and 15 000 people were in attendance. Archie Gumede and Albertina Sisulu were elected to the presidency. And the NIC's Mewa Ramgobin was one of the two individuals who served as the treasurer. With the NIC well represented on the UDF's executive, and with its services for Natal already well in place, the UDF was ready to co-ordinate its immediate objective, namely to organise the boycott of the August elections. Beyond that, the UDF was to continue its efforts to ensure the rejection of state-imposed institutions nationally and locally.[20]

As an organisation within the UDF, the NIC launched an intense anti-constitution campaign in the months before the election. It had already established links with local organisations and action groups, whose services would be valuable. The campaign took many forms, but public meetings provided the most effective forums in which the anti-constitution debates could be conducted. The public meetings were well advertised, and often the organisers transported hundreds of supporters to these gatherings. Some of the more important meetings attracted crowds in their thousands.

These public meetings were extraordinary events, full of rhetoric and emotion. Speakers and audiences participated in spirited rallies against the government. The meetings were

highly charged as the anti-constitution forces reaffirmed their
beliefs, and in that way created a moment in time in which
they felt a sense of triumph. The meetings recharged their
spirits, and the crowds came away with a firmer dedication to
and belief in the efficacy of the politics of refusal. To many
supporters, the 1981 anti-SAIC campaign was being replayed
on a much larger scale for bigger stakes.

It may be instructive to examine four such public meetings
for which detailed transcripts exist, thanks to the electronic
surveillance of the South African security police.[21] The meetings were held at the Stonebridge Community Hall in Phoenix
on 11 December 1983; at the Stardust Cinema, Marburg, Port
Shepstone on 22 July 1984; at the Ladysmith Indian Civic
Centre on 1 August 1984; and at the Newcastle Indian Civic
Hall on 18 August 1984.

The speakers at these meetings were usually carefully
selected for their national and local prominence.[22] Speakers
who had experienced detention and arrest were important for
the sense of sacrifice that they conveyed. Individuals with
affiliation to strong religious and civic organisations were
important to the NIC, especially if they brought a message
from their members. At the Ladysmith meeting, for example,
Ebrahim Bawa relayed the anti-constitution stand of a powerful Islamic body in South Africa. And at the Newcastle meeting, Manibhen Sita's presence had great symbolic value: she
was the daughter of Nana Sita, a prominent passive resister in
the Transvaal in the 1940s and 1950s. The presence of local
leaders was important to the NIC. Thus, for example, Richard
Gumede, a leader of the Joint Rent Action Committee, represented the concerns of one of Natal's urban African residential
areas, Hambanati. Other organisations, such as for example,
the Transvaal Indian Congress (TIC) revived in May 1983,
were represented. The TIC president, Dr E. E. Jassat, also
represented the Transvaal Anti-Constitution Committee at the
Newcastle meeting.[23] And, of course, NIC and UDF leadership
was usually well represented at all the meetings.

The issues addressed at these meetings are fairly representative of those raised throughout the campaign by the anti-constitution forces. Was the new constitutional dispensation a genuine step in the right direction leading to the end of white supremacy? Many speakers pointed out quite correctly that the new system did not give the coloureds and Indians effective power. The white-initiated modification of the system was aimed at co-opting the two minorities into maintaining white power and domination. Speaker after speaker warned that greater sectionalisation in South African politics would have disastrous consequences. Coloureds and Indians would simply become junior partners in the implementation of apartheid. 'What kind of friends are we,' asked Ebrahim Bawa speaking for the Islamic Council of South Africa, 'if we are coparticipants in an oppressive system that oppressed Africans.'[24]

The exclusion of Africans, of course, was to many a clear indication of the real purpose behind the proposed changes. M. J. Naidoo said that they would lock the country into a new system of white privilege and power to hold back the Africans. Fatima Meer warned that the new constitution was a 'dangerous weapon', a 'sword of apartheid', on which the Indians and coloureds were being asked to impale themselves. Her use of the word 'straitjacket' implied that there would be little room for the Indians and coloureds to act independently of apartheid's agenda. This fear of being manipulated expressed itself in the belief that the acceptance of the constitution would result in forced conscription into the army. Mewa Ramgobin saw the constitution as part of the government's 'total strategy' that depended upon increased militarisation. 'This faked vote, this faked ballot box will in fact facilitate the government to give us real bullets to kill our own people', he said.[25]

Although those who had opted to serve in the new system had become the butt of ridicule, most speakers pointed out that in a flawed plan, the quality of the people working in it was not an issue. The car had no engine in it, is the way Farouk Meer put it, and it did not matter who the driver was. Those who promised to be 'tigers' in the new parliament, could be nothing more than 'lambs'. Allan Boesak was much more forthright in his assessment: those who served in a 'thoroughly evil' system – 'haraam' and 'heresy' were words he used – would be committing blasphemy, he implied.[26]

Something of the spirit of the meeting is apparent in the detailed, verbatim transcripts. At the Phoenix meeting, for example, freedom songs were sung. The master of ceremonies, Paul David, used many dramatic gestures to maintain enthusiasm among the audience: he introduced the speakers one by one as they appeared on the stage; and between pauses poetry was read, songs sung, or 'Raj' jokes related.[27]

On 22 August, 29.5 per cent of the coloured registered voters cast their ballots. The Labour Party of Allan Hendrikse won 76 of the 80 seats. As for the Indians who voted on 28 August, just over 20 per cent of the registered voters (or 16.2 per cent of all those who were eligible) participated in the elections. Amichand Rajbansi's National People's Party was the majority party with 23 seats followed by the Solidarity Party with 19. P.W. Botha was elected by an electoral college as the president. A new President's Council was put into place. Its 60 members were distributed as follows: 41 whites of whom 35 were affiliated to the ruling National Party, 13 coloureds, and 6 Indians. Hendrikse and Rajbansi were selected to serve on the government's cabinet. On 25 January 1985, Botha opened the first session of the tricameral parliament.

Even as the new system was being put into place, the UDF had stepped up its campaign against it. Its call for the rejection of state-imposed institutions found its mark. Early in September 1984, the Vaal triangle exploded into popular uprisings. The defiance was widespread, and was to influence other parts of the country as well. In the Vaal triangle, some 800 000 boycotting scholars joined the movement. In the same month, the action of six UDF and NIC leaders captured national and international attention. They took refuge in the British consulate in Durban. Five of the six had just been released from detention, after the Supreme Court had found their incarceration illegal. The action was to focus world attention on the policy of political detention, but most especially to point to the failure of the dialogue instituted by President Ronald Reagan and Prime Minister Margaret Thatcher in their dealings with the apartheid regime.[28]

The state of rebellion was to continue almost unabated through to 1986. Early in 1985, the unrest spread elsewhere: to the East Rand and Pretoria, to the eastern and western Cape, and to Natal as well. Civic organisations in the black townships organised rent boycotts to cripple the administrative capacities of apartheid-imposed local authorities; and they used consumer boycotts against white businesses to exercise on them the kind of political pressures they had never felt before. Students at black schools and universities, who throughout the 1970s had developed a culture of resistance through a variety of forums, broadened their critique to include the whole system, as is apparent in their slogan 'Liberation before Education'. But perhaps the most significant development in the challenge to the state was the rise of black trade unions. Black trade unions were developing rapidly in the 1970s, until the government was forced to extend to them legal recognition in the early 1980s. By 1985, the Congress of South African Trade Unions (COSATU) had emerged as an umbrella organisation representing 33 unions with a membership of 450 000. COSATU generally supported the stand of community organisations.

In the steady drift towards a civil war, the state attempted to win back control though heavy-handed repression using legal and extralegal methods. Arrest and detention of popular leaders, among them UDF persons, kidnapping and assassination of activists, destabilisation and destruction of communities sometimes through the use of black vigilante forces, were tactics used by the government. These tactics certainly blunted the edge of the anti-government forces, but the state was unable to dislodge the yard, street, and area committees that had come to fill the vacuum left by the collapsing local authorities created by the apartheid regime. Anti-apartheid forces could claim the creation of 'liberation zones' in areas in which the state was denied authority.[29]

*Revival and Resurgence*


Throughout all this, the NIC continued its policy of working through local organisations, or specially created bodies, in an attempt to build grass roots support. It certainly used the concept of street and area committees. But the struggle in the Indian areas was nowhere near as intense as in the African areas, which bore the brunt of the government's assault. As an affiliate of the UDF, the NIC's activities in Natal brought it into conflict with Chief Mangosuthu Buthelezi and Inkatha. The death of Victoria Mxenge, a lawyer who defended the UDF leaders accused of high treason, heightened the tensions as rumours mounted about Inkatha's complicity. These tensions, and the UDF-Inkatha clashes in places like Kwa Mashu to the north of Durban, were to manifest themselves in hundreds of Indian families fleeing Inanda, where they had lived for decades. In the attacks that occurred in this area, vandals are said to have destroyed buildings at the Phoenix Settlement, founded in 1904 by Gandhi, the consequence of the 'ever-increasing degrees of poverty and deprivation' in the region, as Heather Hughes pointed out. The isolated and sporadic instances of violence between the UDF and Inkatha supporters threatened the unity that had been forged between the anti-apartheid forces. The NIC was concerned enough to place a full-page political advertisement in the *Sunday Tribune* on 11 August 1985, under the banner, 'We Want Peace and Friendship. Indians, Africans, & Coloureds Unite! Stay Calm. Don't Let Them Divide Us!', and appealed for political unity with 'our African brothers in the UDF'. But it is possible that the NIC lost support over its inability to stop the violence and the displacement.[30]

The UDF itself faced internal divisions, which were caused by various factors, among them the perception that a 'cabal' of high-ranking NIC leaders had hijacked the organisation, and the reappearance in 1987 of an old issue: whether to pursue its struggle from within by contesting state-run elections or to continue as before. The UDF opted to continue with its politics of refusal. That these were effective is indicated by government action in February 1988, when the UDF and seventeen of its most important affiliates were banned by the regime. It resurfaced as the Mass Democratic Movement (MDM) to campaign against participation in elections on 26 October 1988 in the black townships. While the government claimed a 25 per cent voter turnout, the actual number may only have been about 5 per cent.[31]

Towards the end of the 1980s, the apartheid regime had reached what Murray calls 'an organic crisis'. Its attempts to deracialise domination had failed to shift the black masses from a revolutionary stance to a co-optive mode; and its efforts to divert resources to improve and upgrade facilities in the black areas – in what was called the WHAM (Win Hearts And Minds) programme – came too late and offered very little. Indeed, the government's failures offered the ANC in exile an opportunity to increasingly identify itself with the struggle. Even though the ANC was a banned organisation, it made its presence felt directly and indirectly by promoting the destruction of apartheid institutions. Together with its allies, as Stephen Davis pointed out, the ANC was able to embed 'in the political terrain a nationwide infrastructure of anti-apartheid resistance'. But it was unable to bring resistance to a climax during the period of insurgency.[32]

The crisis on the domestic front was accompanied by an increasingly hostile international environment. Serious doubts about the long-term viability of white minority rule had begun to be entertained after the 1976 Soweto uprisings, and they grew significantly in the 1980s among foreign investors. The total loss of capital from all sources between 1984 and 1987 is estimated at R25.2 billion. Trade and military sanctions came into place even in countries like the United States and Britain, where the Reagan administration and the Thatcher government had resisted them. Indeed, by the end of 1986, South Africa had been 'effectively cut off from the international capital market . . .'[33] In its efforts to deny the ANC bases in neighbouring countries, the Pretoria government had used its military power to destabilise them directly by launching raids, or indirectly by supporting surrogates. These countries

responded by using their diplomatic influence in the Commonwealth, and other forums, to further censure South Africa. In
any event, the ANC had become firmly entrenched inside
South Africa, as became apparent from the growing number of
its military attacks: 230 in 1986, 235 in 1987, and 281 in
1988.[34]

By 1988, the National Party faced a serious crisis of confidence in its leadership. P.W. Botha, who had come to rely
heavily on the 'securocrats' in the State Security Council,
stubbornly clung to military rather than bold political solutions. The momentum for initiating some form of negotiation
with the ANC was building up even among his own supporters,
as was evident from the number of private delegations that
visited Lusaka in Zambia to meet with the outlawed organisation.[35] Botha suffered a stroke, and his hold on the party
leadership became even more tenuous. F.W. de Klerk, long in
the government, emerged to challenge Botha and assumed the
leadership. The erosion of white support for the National Party
was apparent in the 1989 election: the party received
48 per cent support, the lowest since it had come to power in
1948. Disaffected Nationalist voters supported the Conservative Party, which received 31 per cent of the popular white
vote.

De Klerk had few options other than to search for political
solutions. He moved on several fronts to end the stalemate:
firstly, he agreed to independence for Namibia to bring an end
to South Africa's military occupation; secondly, he released
from detention MDM's 'Terror' Lekota and Popo Molefe, and
Rivonia trialists Walter Sisulu, Ahmed Kathrada, Andrew
Mlangeni, Elias Motsoaledi, Raymond Mhlaba, and Wilton
Mkwayi; thirdly, he unbanned on 2 February 1990, the ANC,
PAC, and SACP, and other organisations to allow their return
to legal political status; and, fourthly, he released Nelson
Mandela on 11 February 1990 unconditionally after twenty-
seven years of imprisonment. These initial steps cleared the
way to the search for political democracy in South Africa.

A new political terrain had emerged by 1990, and the UDF –

## CHAPTER 8

# Conclusion

In its journey from 1894 to the present, the NIC has experienced a remarkable change. Starting out with narrowly conceived goals and restricted membership, it went from constitutionalism to direct action. Its objectives broadened from concessionary privileges to inherent rights, and from ethnocentrism to non-racialism. The organisation's earlier commercially based leaders gave way to individuals from professional and working-class backgrounds. These changes are to be seen in the context, firstly, of the transformations among the Indians themselves and, secondly, in that of the unyielding nature of white supremacy from its incipient form in the nineteenth century to its fully developed apartheid manifestation in the twentieth century.

To recapitulate briefly, the NIC was founded in 1894 at the instigation of M.K. Gandhi, who played an influential but not a central role in the organisation's early years. The body's agenda was shaped largely by the commercial élite that dominated its leadership, and when its interests were threatened by a political campaign with an enlarged scope, it broke with Gandhi and his supporters in 1913. For the next seven years, the NIC virtually ceased to exist. It was revived in 1921, and committed itself to a course in which it accepted the mediatory role of the diplomatic representative of the Government of India. The NIC leaders weathered several crises in their search for a resolution of issues within the imperial context over the next twenty-five years. In the end they failed, and their place was taken by a new brand of

leaders who were militant in their defiance of white supremacy. They launched a passive resistance campaign in 1946,
and built an organisational alliance with the ANC. The
alliance was shattered, however, after the government
banned the ANC in 1960. After 1961, the NIC ceased to exist
until it was revived in 1971. In the two decades after that,
the NIC placed itself firmly within the fold of the larger
liberation movement. The NIC resisted the racialisation
process of the apartheid years through non-cooperation. It
espoused non-racialism, and assumed a 'black' identity without, however, adopting a programme to reverse the demoni-
sation of the African 'other'. This study has dwelt on these
developments.

In reflecting upon its journey, I consider three broadly
interrelated questions. One, the essentiality of the ethnic
identities among the Indians, and how they manifested themselves. Two, how the NIC built its support given the enormous
diversity among its constituents. And, three, the extent to
which the NIC succeeded in the post-1945 period, but
especially after 1971, in promoting non-racialism among the
thousands who attended its rallies.

Indians, from the beginning, have created voluntary and
semi-voluntary organisations. What Gary D. Klein discovered
about a small sample of Gujarati Indians is probably true of all
groups of South Africa's Indians. Exclusively ethnic, religious
or caste group formation was a way of maintaining internal
cohesion.[1] As a young man growing up in the 1940s and 1950s,
I was socialised into accepting the group loyalty of the subcaste association of which I was an involuntary member. The
association's leaders sought to confine all the activities of its
young men and women within the group, but were unable to
control their affiliation to other organisations in which membership was inclusive. The power of the leaders had eroded in
an environment in which there were greater areas of voluntary
choice. This was particularly true of sporting bodies. A variety
of factors was to break down the internal cohesion with time.
But I was struck by how strong the group loyalties had been –

*Conclusion*

and in many cases still are – when the sub-caste associations flourished.

It was as I was examining the columns of the *Indian Opinion* and *Indian Views* for the 1920s, 1930s, and 1940s, that I discovered how prevalent religious and cultural organisations had been in the early period. I returned to the issues covering some of the years to examine them more carefully for cultural activities. These newspapers served to some extent as bulletin boards for their community of readers. Sporting activities, cultural events, religious festivals, and even commercial advertisements, were important indicators of how Indians were engaged outside of politics and the workplace. Since these reported events represented only a portion of the totality of such activities, I was struck by how significant they were. This encouraged me to examine such activities in the *Leader* in the later period between 1974 and 1984. My research only confirmed what I had instinctively known all along, namely, Indian identities are considerably shaped by the cultural and religious heritage of Indians under altered circumstances, and they have persisted even as they became South Africanised. This process affected every aspect of the South African Indian experience, including politics. No scholarly account can ignore the process. I examine briefly the cultural/religious activities for the period before 1950, and for the 1970s and 1980s.

Before 1950, religion was clearly the most important force in the lives of the Indians. HYMA, founded in 1905, met annually, and hosted guests from India. The Arya Pratinidhi Sabha promoted Hinduism through Vedic conferences. The Sanatan Dharma Sabha held discussions yearly on the Bhagvad Gita. The South African Hindu Maha Sabha in the 1930s attempted to serve as an umbrella organisation. These and local Hindu temple organisations all over Natal annually celebrated religious festivals. What is interesting is that often the same organisations were involved in promoting vernacular languages: Hindi, Tamil, Telegu, and Gujarati. The Hari Bhajan Sadbakta in 1891 was the first to do so. In January 1918, about twenty such organisations met in Pietermaritzburg to promote vernacular education. In 1952, the Hindi Shiksa Sangh of Natal met in Pietermaritzburg to do the same.[2] Islam was important to Muslim Indians, and they promoted the religion through a variety of organisations: Anjuman Islam, Young Muslim Association, Muslim Debating Society, Muslim Youth League, and Muslim Young Men's Association. In 1935, the first Muslim Conference was held at the Jumma Mosque in Grey Street. For the Parsis, the Zoroastrian Anjuman was important; and the small Indian Christian community was very active through a variety of churches. The *Indian Opinion* and *Indian Views* ran regular features on religion, especially Hinduism and Islam.

While religion was the most important marker of ethnic identity, it incorporated broadly a 'cultural' element as well. Nevertheless, there were organisations that specifically promoted 'culture'. Whether they were secular or religious, there was an Indianness to them, both in their activities and in their membership. The range of such organisations was extraordinarily broad. There were, for example, the Mayville Indian Youngmen's Society, Gyaan Prachar Natak Mundal, Gujarati Youngmen's Society, Natal Muslim Educational Committee, Crescent Debating Society, Karnatic Music Society, Clairwood Literary and Debating Club, and Durban Indian Women's Association.

Between 1921 and 1936, I found reference to at least a dozen plays. In 1921, for example, the Saraswathee Samarsa Sungeetha Drama Company produced 'Markandiar'. Music and literature were important components of culture. Weekly, the newspapers carried commercial advertisements for the latest music albums and books. Nothing, however, was to make as dramatic a cultural impact as 'talking' movies. The film industry hit Durban in the 1940s, and since then the appetite for screen heroes like Renuka Devi, Leela Chitnis, and Ashok Kumar has seemed insatiable. Movie theatres sprang up all over Durban.

Sporting activities became important, and every sport was followed with interest. Cricket, football, boxing, and wrestling

*Conclusion*

were the most popular sports. Local boxers like Seaman Chetty and Tiger Shaik were followed with interest. When sportsmen came from overseas interest reached phenomenal heights. This was the case when Mottee (Kid) Singh, a boxer from England, and Ali Bey, an Egyptian wrestler, visited South Africa in 1933 and 1935. Sports, like other activities among the Indians, were organised along sectional or secular lines. There were bodies, such as the Bharat Cricket Club, Verulam Hindu Football (also Cricket) Club, and the Muslim Cricket Club, which had a religiously defined membership. I am not sure about clubs like the Ottoman, Overport, Pirates, Kismet, and others. But some clubs, among them the Teachers Cricket Club, Indian Bicycling Club, All Black Football Club, and those football clubs that participated in the Sam China Tournament opened their membership to all Indians non-sectionally. Occasionally, Indian clubs played against white clubs.

The picture that emerges, then, is one of a culture- and religion-centredness that is multiply diverse for the period before the 1950s. Indians identified themselves as 'Indians' as a consequence of the historical circumstances that created that category in the 1890s and beyond – it was imposed by the politically dominant group, but it was also adopted for convenience. But beyond that label, 'Indians' were Hindus or Muslims, Gujaratis or 'Madrasis' in situations in which culture, religion, and even language, were more important indicators of ethnic boundaries.

By the 1970s and 1980s, all classes of Indians had experienced upward social and economic mobility. A professional élite had emerged. Group areas legislation had uprooted thousands of families, but it had also provided low-cost housing to many who would not otherwise have had their own homes. The apartheid state had expanded segregated educational facilities, and many had access to secondary and tertiary education. The Indian population in Natal generally became more fluent English speakers as their facility in the vernacular languages weakened or became non-existent. They read English-language daily newspapers. Their political awareness became more informed and sophisticated, even if they were excluded from the system. Even in the midst of apartheid-generated demons, there was talk about democracy and non-racialism among many groups of Indians. They were more Westernised, and secular in their thinking than ever before.

Yet in the midst of all of this, the cultural and religious indicators as reflected in *Leader* are as strong as ever, and the participation of Indians generally in these activities goes beyond symbolic tokenism. The Ved Dharma Sabha, the Arya Pratinidhi Sabha, Andhra Maha Sabha, and the South African Hindu Maha Sabha, among others, are still actively promoting Hinduism through annual religious festivals. The Kavady festival continues to attract thousands of devotees annually. Muslim groups are equally active, as are the Indian Christian churches. The groups promote vernacular languages, religion, and culture by organising events and inviting prominent guests from India. I noticed that almost every year up to the early 1980s, when the cultural boycott movement made its appearance, there were swamis, singers, dancers, and actors travelling from India, and elsewhere. There was something like a spiritual revival as temples, mosques, and churches, as well as local organisations, stepped up their activities.

During the 1970s television made its appearance in South Africa. Yet even with the easy access to Hollywood-produced movies provided by this medium, about a dozen cinemas in Durban weekly featured movies from India. Zeenat Aman, Saira Banu, Hema Malini, Rajesh Khanna, Dharmendra, and Amitabh Bachchan were the north-Indian screen idols, while Sivaji Ganesh was the all-time favourite in Tamil films. Quawali singers from Pakistan and elsewhere entertained traditional audiences, as did Pithikuli Murugadas. But local music groups organised Durban performers in musical festivals at which orchestras were composed of combined Western and Eastern instruments. Radio Truro, established in 1976, and later Radio Lotus, blared Indian music daily to avid listeners. Classical dancing and yoga schools were well patro-

*Conclusion*

nised. Sporting activities had increased, and while most organisations were confined to Indian membership, they subscribed to the non-racial philosophy of the South African Council of Sports (SACOS). I am not sure how much religious or cultural exclusivity was retained from club to club, but they all participated in regionally based competitions.

While some of this is what the anthropologists might call symbolic forms of ethnicity, one cannot dismiss the entire range of cultural and religious activities as being insignificant. They are important in defining the identities of South African Indians in their many diverse forms.

Given this enormous diversity of class, caste, religion, and culture, how did the NIC build a base of support for itself? M. K. Gandhi carefully cultivated, as was discussed in chapter two, the support of the leaders within the separate cultural or religious organisations. While maintaining their identities in their respective bodies, they accepted the benefit of assuming a new political identity as 'Indians' under the leadership of the NIC. They lost nothing by doing so. They were not required to give up their affiliation to the bodies from which their fundamental sense of identity came. When Gopal K. Gokhale visited South Africa in 1912, upon Gandhi's invitation, seventeen organisations separately sent him welcome messages. Of the seventeen, eight had religious orientations, but the general reception committee had representatives from many of them.

Far more numerous were the caste and subcaste group organisations among the Hindus. Two of these were the Patidar Society in Johannesburg and the Koli Hitvardhak Mandal. There were many among other subcaste groups: Anavils, Durjis, Khatris, Suthars, Mochis. There were, no doubt, such subcaste organisations among those of south Indian ancestry, whose membership was proscriptive.

Secular bodies were to emerge in every sphere of Indian activity, and their membership would be inclusive. A few examples would be: the Natal Indian Blind Society, Natal Indian Boy Scouts Association, and the Merebank Literary and Debating Society. In sports, the Dundee United Cricket Club and the Newcastle Indian Football Association are good examples. And in trade unions, the SAR and H Indian Employees' Union and the Indian Farmers' Union serve well to illustrate the point.

I found few instances where such ethnic, religious, and subcaste group divisions were used for political representation, although it did happen. A BIA deputation that went to see the Minister of the Interior in 1916 had representation from the Patidars, Kolis, Indian Christians, the Colonial-born Indian Association, and the Transvaal Indian Mahomedan Congress. And in March 1917, the Durban mayor received an eight-person deputation about raising war-related charity funds. The eight persons represented: Christian Indians, Calcutta Hindus, Parsis, Madras Hindus, Bombay Hindus, Bombay Muslims, Madras Muslims, and Calcutta Muslims.[3]

In examining the non-secular affiliations of people who made up the NIC leadership, it is clear that they had deep and fundamental ties with cultural and religious bodies. Thus Kajee was a patron of the Muslim Institute and a member of the Nizamia Muslim Society; Amra, a member of the National-ist Bloc and the CPSA, was on the committee of the Muslim Institute; Lawrence was closely associated with organisations of the Catholic Indian community; Monty Naicker started out as a president in 1936 of the Hindu Youth League; S.R. Naidoo was a secretary of Hari Bhajan Sadbakta Saara Sangraha in Cato Manor; P.R. Pather was a member of the Hindu Tamil Institute from 1918 to 1951; and V.S.C. Pather was an impor-tant member of the Arya Pratinidhi Sabha in Durban. These individuals moved in more than one community.

What emerges from this is that Indian leaders were fully aware of the cultural and religious diversity of the people they hoped to serve; and in their selection of the executive and committee members of the NIC, or any other secular body for that matter, they took full cognisance of this fact. For example, in 1935, the Indian Hospital Advisory Committee was appointed. The membership reflects a broad representa-tion: E.M. Paruk, V.S.C. Pather, S.G. Randeria, V. Lawrence,

*Conclusion*

Hans Maghrajh, S. Rustomjee, A. Christopher, B.M. Patel, and M.C. Bassa. In 1921, when the NIC was revived, there were one president, six vice-presidents, two joint secretaries, two joint treasurers, and twenty-four committee members. There was a clear attempt to balance the NIC executive among all the diverse constituencies. Some of this balance disappeared with the colonisation issue in the 1930s, when those of indentured heritage felt betrayed. Regional and racial differences surfaced as the tensions increased; S.M. Nana even called the CBSIA supporters 'kolchas' ('coals', meaning roughly 'darkies' or it could have been a corrupt form of 'coolies'). The representational imbalance was corrected somewhat by 1940; but new class divisions appeared with the perception that the Kajee-Pather group represented mainly the wealthy element. The progressive leadership of the post-1945 period remained alive to the newer constituencies, but even they were careful not to slight the diversity of the Indians in the composition of the executive. I.C. Meer recalled that Gopalal Hurbans was included on the executive because he had the support of many in Tongaat.[4]

It is clear that at least up to the 1950s, the NIC's success as a secular, inclusive, political organisation depended on the body's maintaining a loose coalition of cultural and religious organisations for its support. Culture and religion are important considerations in these six decades; and despite the extent to which secularisation occurred to create a more inclusive type of association, they are both vital ingredients in the way in which ethnicity was defined and redefined.

In sociological terms, intergroup and intragroup relations among Indians were in a constant dialectical process of change in which ethnic boundaries were being renewed through absorption of the 'other', co-operation or conflict, and assimilation. Even in instances where in-group loyalties were shaped by biological and ancestral concerns, members responded to external forces in the form of social and economic opportunities, and in that way redefined themselves ethnically.

An urban working-class Indian population had emerged by the 1940s, and it was increasingly exposed to a non-racial ideology by NIC leaders who were trade-unionists and/or SACP members. The class dimension made a strong appearance in NIC politics, and it served to promote the idea of a non-racial alliance of organisations, but it did not eliminate the ethnic self-perception of the NIC or its members. It added another expression of identification, not quite replacing the old, but giving a new definition to what was already there.

The trends that were apparent by 1960 resurfaced strongly when the NIC was revived in 1971. The NIC leaders were educated and articulate, and were informed by an ideology that was not necessarily new and a strategy that was clearer in its vision. Having reaffirmed their belief in non-racialism, and having aligned the NIC with other non-racial organisations, the leaders sought to develop support among Indian civic, welfare, and labour bodies. I am not sure whether the NIC targeted cultural and religious organisations, but it did not exclude them in its coalition of support groups. It welcomed, for example, the support of the Islamic Council of South Africa in its fight against the 1984 constitution. As a member of the UDF, the NIC was part of a much larger movement that incorporated all other bodies whose goal was to destroy apartheid. The NIC was Indian in its composition, but increasingly used the term 'black' to describe itself as a way to reaffirm its commitment to the forces opposing apartheid. The one point of difference between the pre- and post-1971 NIC is that the latter was less concerned, if at all, with having the balance on its executive reflect the cultural and religious diversity of Indians. It concentrated on drawing from bodies that were secularised and inclusive, and in a stronger position to affect the infrastructure of white minority rule. The NIC may not have had traditional membership lists, but it was always able to attract thousands to its rallies when the need arose. It had the support of the secularised bodies I referred to, as well as of the youth who made up a significantly large percentage.

How well has the NIC succeeded in promoting non-racialism? The answer resides in the way in which the NIC has fared in two broad objectives it set for itself after 1971: first, to prevent Indians from being absorbed into state-created apartheid political structures; and, second, to inculcate democratic values among its constituents.

In its drive to prevent Indians from electorally endorsing government structures, the NIC undertook a massive door-to-door campaign with the help of area and regional committees, which ironically eclipsed the organisation's branches.[5] The NIC was one among several bodies that constituted a 'culture of liberation', and contributed to what Price calls issue-linkage, namely the interconnectedness, for example, between the workplace and residence in the overall system of white domination.[6] But there was weakness in the very thing in which the NIC was successful. As R. Singh and S. Vawda have pointed out, the NIC's political mobilisation occurred 'within terms of apartheid reality'. There was 'space' within 'apartheid hegemony' to destabilise that reality. But the NIC failed to capitalise on it.[7] What is implied in this criticism is that the NIC should have set its own parameters within which to discredit apartheid while at the same time promoting democratic values. Perhaps its forums and constituencies should have been less Indian and more non-racial. Or, to put it differently, the NIC embraced non-racialism within a racial context.

The NIC's failure to propagate democratic values effectively was the consequence of not having established an entrenched, broadly based constituency. Its own internal mechanism became increasingly narrow, and this caused disaffection among regional activists who felt excluded from decisions made by the central executive. Some of these issues were debated in two NIC workshops organised in 1987 or 1988. The NIC needed greater internal democracy if it was to work effectively. It did not see any difficulty with its ethnic composition so long as the organisation was 'rooted in the concrete conditions of the Indian community' and was able to build a base of mass support.[8]

Much was written in the newspapers about the 'cabal' in the NIC. The word has been used to suggest that a coterie of individuals manipulated events behind the scenes. Now that more information is available, as more persons are forthcoming

*Gandhi's Legacy*

with details about the NIC, it is possible to place the issue within a proper historical perspective. On the surface, the issue reflected, as Ela Gandhi explained, two approaches: the realistic one that argued for greater community participation, and the romantic perception that held that an executive high profile was all that was necessary to keep up the liberation momentum in the 1980s. The issue goes much deeper, however. A group of individuals, some of whom may have been informed by Lenin's notion of vanguard leadership, took it upon themselves to chart a different course of action for the NIC. These persons believed that the old style of leadership – open forums, and the like – was no longer effective. They had contact and communication, it seems, with underground liberation organisations; in addition, they had access to overseas funds, which were to be used, among other things, in the defence of anti-apartheid activists. All of this gave them the confidence to plan and implement effective strategies without reference to open, democratic procedures, and to work through trusted key individuals and organisations in and around Durban. Many in the NIC felt excluded. M.J. Naidoo recalled how the group was able to organise a closed election of NIC officials in 1987 at a meeting held in Chatsworth in a cloak-and-dagger fashion. While the individuals may have considered this necessary in the repressive decade of the 1980s, many NIC supporters and officials saw their action as cabalistic. Some of those identified as part of the cabal are now members of the National Parliament. In time, they will write about their activities in the 1970s and 1980s.[9]

Whatever its shortcomings in the late 1980s, one cannot deny the NIC's very important role in preventing co-option in 1981 and 1984. The NIC pointed to the perils of participating in ethnic politics at the expense of the African majority. In promoting the ideals of the Freedom Charter, the NIC was in a sense advancing the cause of the ANC as well. Only time will tell how much of this was based on instructions from banned organisations such as the ANC and SACP.

Perhaps owing to the NIC's weaknesses and the newer

realities after 1990, there has been at least one major resignation from the organisation. Mewa Ramgobin, who held the NIC
vice-presidency, resigned in 1992. The NIC had done well in
keeping alive the Freedom Charter since 1971, he acknowledged, but with the ANC back on the scene, that commitment
could no longer be advanced on 'racial or ethnic lines'. Besides,
the NIC had virtually ceased to exist, he said. The last
conference had been held in 1987, and branches had disappeared. But the NIC's secretary, Farouk Meer, believed otherwise. Meer insisted that the NIC had a role to play in frus-
trating the National Party's efforts to court Indian support.[10]

That there should have been fears about Indians supporting
De Klerk's National Party, which had been responsible for
apartheid, suggests perhaps that the NIC's influence had been
less than effective among some elements. Even in places like
Chatsworth and Phoenix, where low-income Indians reside, the
initial analysis of the first democratic election in 1994 showed
strong support for the National Party. As Adam Habib, an
academic, said in 1993, 'It is partly the result of the apartheid
legacy – the sowing of distrust between Indians and Africans –
and partly a product of the failure of the liberation movement to
address adequately the ethnic question.'[11] Apartheid demonised
African majority rule, and many Indians have yet to recover
from the fear and suspicion this process has sown. Ethnically
inspired fears have grown among them. It should not be
forgotten that when Gandhi founded the NIC in 1894, it was to
persuade the whites that Indians were superior to the 'Kaffir'
other. That attitude did not disappear in the 1920s and 1930s,
and lingered in some form even beyond the 1950s. It seems that
the network of religious and cultural organisations has grown
stronger with the uncertainties of the last decade. The temples,
mosques, and churches that define ethnic boundaries continue
to be well patronised. The ANC recognised this and targeted
such bodies in its electoral campaign. At a 1992 meeting in
Chatsworth addressed by Nelson Mandela, 150 local organisations were represented. The ANC hoped to reach the Hindu
Maha Sabha, the Aryan Benevolent Home, the Tamil Protection

Association, among others, according to one of its high ranking members.[12]

The NIC's campaign against racial exclusiveness alerted Indians, even those who were only peripherally interested in NIC activities, to its dangers. The NIC held out a vision of a non-racial South Africa with which many could identify. And in this, the NIC's work was commendable.

But beyond that, the NIC remained a movement which was unable to sustain a network of allies. In the last few years its structures remained too centralised, and its leadership much too removed from the rank and file to build a base of mass support. Having to answer to an ill-defined, loose constituency of supporters, the leaders did not face the rigours of accountability. They tended, therefore, to impose from above rather than structure from below through the medium of 'town hall' type meetings. It appears, then, that the NIC failed to maintain its programme to educate Indians on the values of democratic rule as an accompaniment to its message of non-racialism.

Some have suggested that the continued existence of the NIC, and also the TIC for that matter, will ensure that Indians as a separate group have high-profile representation in an African-dominated government. This sentiment reflects, in part, the apartheid-bred concept of ethnic political representation implying that members of an ethnic group, the Indians in this case, can best represent its own interests. It is also rooted in the history of the NIC itself. For much of its one hundred years of existence, both the membership and the issues remained Indian-oriented, a situation which was imposed by the white power structure. The current fear, it seems to me, is that despite the reassurances by the ANC, the Indians as a minority group will be neglected in the reallocation of resources in an apartheid-free South Africa. They expect affirmative action favouring Africans to affect them adversely. Those who think in this manner hope that the NIC will ensure that this does not happen, but as far as I have been able to determine, they have no clear idea as to what kind of body the NIC should become.

*Conclusion*

At the moment, Indians do play a fairly significant role in the ANC, and many are now part of the newly elected National Assembly as ANC members. Indians hold important positions in the new ANC government, and will have some influence in decision-making in the immediate future. But they, like the whites, will have to recognise that redressing the inequities of the past is essential to securing lasting democratic rule.

There has been a debate about converting the NIC into a cultural body. However this new role is defined, the reconstituted NIC would seek to place under its umbrella the diverse elements of the cultures, religions, and languages that make up the South Africa Indian communities today. Indeed, the NIC may then become a focal point of common cultural aspects that bind the people of Indian ancestry rather than those that separate and divide them. But this may be a difficult task given the reality that Indians are affiliated to many diverse organisations that appear to fulfil their most fundamental needs. The challenge for the South African Indians remains to develop a political culture that will facilitate their incorporation into a non-racial South Africa without necessarily giving up their affiliation to ethnically defined organisations. If the NIC can play a role in this, it has a future.

Does the NIC have a role to play beyond its centenary? Its centenary celebration in August 1994 was a pretty dismal affair. Only 150 people were present and the NIC president George Sewpersadh left before he could be honoured with a citation for his contributions. NIC secretary, Farouk Meer, insisted that the organisation had a role to play beyond 1994 if it could 'rejuvenate' itself. In this process of rejuvenation, the NIC will have to determine in what sense it seeks to represent Indians. It needs to be aware of the strategic value of Indianness and to operate in such a way as to be always conscious of the intersecting axes of continuity and of falsity that frame Indianness. It needs to locate all identity in its historical context. The shape of identity is in the process of being redefined and we need to be wary of moves that will reiterate the ideological underpinnings of apartheid. 'Indianness' as a basis of politics has

## Chapter 1
## Introduction: An Overview of the Natal Indian Congress

1. T.K. Mahadevan's *The Year of the Phoenix: Not a Novel*, New Delhi, 1982, presents Gandhi as a calculatingly ambitious person, and argues that he knew about the bill for some time, and not just at the last minute as he claimed in his autobiography. Gandhi read the newspapers regularly, and avidly collected a scrapbook of articles from them, Mahadevan maintains.
2. See E.S. Reddy and G. Gandhi (eds), *Gandhi and South Africa*, Ahmedabad: Navajivan, 1993.
3. See Surendra Bhana and Joy Brain, *Setting Down Roots: Indian Migrants in South Africa, 1860–1911*, Johannesburg: Witwatersrand University Press, 1990, and Surendra Bhana, *Indentured Indian Emigrants to Natal, 1860–1902: A Study Based on Ships' Lists*, New Delhi: Promilla and Co., 1991.

## Chapter 2
## The Search for Imperial Brotherhood: 1894–1914

1. For a list of the members see the 1894 Natal Indian Congress report in the *The Collected Works of Mahatma Gandhi*, Delhi: Government of India, 1958– (hereafter *CWMG*), I, pp. 162–65.
2. An individual wrote a letter to the newspaper accusing Gandhi of being paid £300 for his secretarial work, which Gandhi refuted. *CWMG*, I, pp. 247–53.
3. *CWMG*, I, p. 320.
4. Ibid., pp. 131–32.
5. 'First Report of the NIC, August, 1895' in *CWMG*, I, pp. 231–39.
6. 'Second Report of the NIC, October 11, 1899' in *CWMG*, III, pp. 96–110. See also Gandhi's autobiography, *The Story of My Experiments with Truth*, Washington: Public Affairs Press, 1948, pp. 185–86.
7. *CWMG*, I, pp. 247–53. The secretary had authority to sign cheques up to £5. All expenses beyond that sum required one other signatory from among six executive members. See *CWMG*, I, p. 233.
8. *CWMG*, III, pp. 203–4.
9. *CWMG*, III, pp. 96–110.
10. *CWMG*, VI, pp. 289–91, 409–10.
11. *CWMG*, IX, pp. 133, 201–2.

12. Maureen Swan, *Gandhi: The South African Experience*, Johannesburg: Ravan, 1985, pp. 2–10.
13. Ibid. See also *CWMG*, VI, pp. 465–67 in which tribute is paid to Omar Haji Jhavery (also Zaveri). For more details on Nazar, see S. Bhana and James D. Hunt, (eds), *Gandhi's Editor: The Letters of M. H. Nazar, 1902–3*, New Delhi: Promilla and Co., 1989.
14. *CWMG*, II, pp. 2–36, 69–91, 104–15; III, pp. 90–110; VI, pp. 207–10; VIII, p. 68; IX, pp. 344–50.
15. See Bhana and Brain, *Setting Down Roots*, and Bhana, *Indentured Indian Emigrants*.
16. *CWMG*, I, pp. 77–81, 92–96, 97–99, 102, 107–11, 116–28.
17. See Bhana and Brain, *Setting Down Roots*, pp. 63–76, 159–87.
18. Swan, *Gandhi*.
19. *CWMG*, III, pp. 113–14, 160; V, p. 349; XI, pp. 108–9.
20. *CWMG*, III, pp. 72–73; IV, pp. 127–28, 136, XI, pp. 162, 179–82, 316.
21. *CWMG*, V, pp. 243–44, 398–99. In a loosely related case, the NIC took an active interest in the Indians who survived the disastrous Lobito Bay scheme, 1907–8. Indians had been recruited to build a railway line in this area of Angola. See *CWMG*, V, p. 369; VIII, pp. 192–93.
22. *CWMG*, V, pp. 234–35; IX, pp. 145–49.
23. Ibid. E. S. Reddy's *Gandhiji: Vision of a Free South Africa*, New Delhi: Sanchar Publishing House, 1955, explores Gandhi's changing attitude toward South Africa's Africans on pp. 19–76.
24. *CWMG*, VI, pp. 409–10.
25. *CWMG*, VII, pp. 113–15.
26. *CWMG*, VIII, p. 472.
27. *CWMG*, VII, p. 98.
28. *CWMG*, VIII, p. 4.
29. *CWMG*, X, p. 213.
30. See *Golden Number of Indian Opinion: Souvenir of the Passive Resistance Movement in South Africa, 1906–1914*, Pietermaritzburg, 1914, pp. 21–26. See *Indian Opinion*, 26 February 1910, and 19 November 1912.
31. Swan, *Gandhi*; J. D. Beall and D. North-Coombes, 'The 1913 Disturbances in Natal: The Social and Economic Background to "Passive Resistance"', *Journal of Natal and Zulu History* 6 (1983), pp. 48–81.
32. *CWMG*, XII, pp. 245–47. The interview appeared in the *Rand Daily Mail*, 23 October 1913. See also *CWMG*, XII, pp. 219–21.
33. *CWMG*, XII, p. 246.
34. Ibid., pp. 245–47.
35. *CWMG*, XII, pp. 274–77. Edwald Esselen and Col. Wylie were unacceptable to the NIA.

36. *CWMG*, XII, p.339.
37. *CWMG*, XII, pp.344–45.
38. In this regard see Swan's *Gandhi*, and her earlier work, 'Ideology in Organised Indian Politics, 1891–1948' in S. Marks and S. Trapido (eds), *The Politics of Race, Class and Nationalism in Twentieth Century South Africa*, New York: Longman, 1987, pp.186–208. She influenced Vishnu Padayachee and Robert Morrell in their article, 'Indian Merchants and Dukawallas in the Natal Economy, c.1875–1914', *Journal of Southern African Studies* 17:1 (March 1991), pp. 71–102.
39. *CWMG*, XII, pp.490–93.
40. Michael Omi and Howard Winant, *Racial Formation in the United States From the 1960s To the 1980s*, New York: Routledge, 1986.

## Chapter 3
## Division and Disillusion: 1920s to 1940s

1. *Indian Opinion*, 12 September 1919. Anglia died on 27 September, twenty days later. See *Indian Opinion*, 3 October 1919.
2. Ibid., 4 September 1925; 17 July 1925.
3. Ibid., 24 December 1920; 11 March 1921.
4. Ibid., 11 March 1921.
5. P.S. Joshi, *The Tyranny of Colour: A Study of the Indian Problem in South Africa*, [Johannesburg: P.S. Joshi] 1942, p.108.
6. Some of the meetings were reported in the *Indian Opinion*. See April and May issues of 1923; 1 February, 7 March 1924; 4 September 1925; 7 and 12 February 1926; 2 and 9 October 1925.
7. The delegation consisted of Dr A. Abdurahman, Amod Bayat, (NIC president), J.W. Godfrey (NIC vice-president), Bhawani Dayal (NIC vice-president), V.S.C. Pather, S. Rustomjee (NIC secretaries), and A.A. Mirza Galibbeg. *Indian Opinion*, 27 November 1925.
8. *Indian Opinion*, 22 October 1926.
9. Ibid., 11 September and 26 November 1926.
10. Ibid., 10 December 1926.
11. Ibid., 26 November 1926; 27 January 1928; 11 December 1931.
12. See Uma S. Mesthrie, 'From Sastri to Deshmukh: A Study of the Role of the Government of India's Representative in South Africa, 1927 to 1946', (Ph.D. Thesis, University of Natal, 1987).
13. *Indian Opinion*, 24 January, 4 and 28 February 1936.
14. *Golden Number of Indian Opinion*, p.29.
15. SAIC Agenda Book: Emergency Conference of the South African Indian Congress, Johannesburg, 5–6 October 1930; Tom Karis's

interview with P.R. Pather, 1964, Carter-Karis collection on microfilm.

16. CBSIA Agenda Book: First Natal Provincial Conference of the Colonial-Born and Settler Indian Association, Durban, 31 December 1933 – 2 January 1934, Carter-Karis collection on microfilm.

17. SAIC Annual Conference, 27 August 1932, Johannesburg; SAIC Emergency Conference, 19–20 August 1933, Johannesburg; SAIC Agenda Book: Fifteenth Annual Conference, 17–18 February 1935, Durban. The Colonisation Commission expected colonisation to be part of a larger scheme in which India would play a role. The government of India, however, had no desire to become involved in such a scheme. Besides, the White Australia policy would have placed British New Guinea off-limits to Asians; and as for British Guiana, the coastal region would have had to be drained and made habitable before any immigrants could be settled there. The commission appeared more desperate than realistic about its proposal. Malaya, Sumatra, Java and the Philippines were considered but ruled out.

18. *Indian Opinion*, 4 February 1938.

19. NIC Agenda Book: Report on Activities from 1 May 1938 to 26 August 1939: submitted to the AGM of the NIC, 27 August 1939, Durban.

20. Ibid., 4 and 25 February 1938, 26 and 27 May 1938, 10, 17 and 24 June 1938, 19 August 1938, 16 December 1938, 24 February, 3 March, 13 October, 3 and 4 November 1939. *Indian Views*, 8 April 1938, 16 December 1938.

21. *Indian Opinion*, 17 February 1939.

22. *Indian Views*, 9 and 16 June 1939, 14 and 28 July 1939.

23. Ibid., 30 August 1939.

24. Ibid., 12 and 19 July 1940, 13 September 1940.

25. Non-European United Front: Conferences, Statements; Minutes of the First Non-European Conference, 23–25 June 1927, Kimberley.

26. The thirteen organisations were: African National Bond, ANC, APO, Bantu Union, Cape Malay Association, Colonial Born Indian Association, Coloured Church, ICU, Indian Political Association (Kimberley), Native Teachers' Association, Negro Universal Improvements Association, SAIC, SA Muslim Association. The SAIC was officially represented by V. Lawrence and A. Ismail. Five other SAIC delegates were present.

27. Non-European United Front: Conferences, Statements; Minutes of the Second Non-European Conference, January 1930, Cape

Town; and Minutes of the Third South African Non-European Conference, 5–8 January 1931, Bloemfontein; Non-European United Front of South Africa, 8–10 April 1939.

28. *Indian Opinion*, 1 December 1939.
29. Ibid., 3 March 1939.
30. *Indian Views*, 2 September 1938; 11 November 1938.
31. SAIC Agenda Book: SAIC Annual Conference, Seventeenth Session, 8–10 February 1946, Johannesburg.
32. NIC Agenda Book: General Meeting, 9 June 1940, Durban; the president was Hajee E.M. Paruk; Hans Maghrajh and Aboobaker Moosa were secretaries; and S.M. Paruk and M.I. Bobat served as joint treasurers. The NIC claimed to have branches in Dannhauser, Vryheid, Dundee, Glencoe, Ladysmith, Estcourt, Pietermaritzburg, Greytown, Isipingo, Port Shepstone, and Durban.
33. NIC Agenda Book: General Meeting, 14 September 1941, Durban.
34. Final Statement submitted by the Natal Indian Association to the Indian Penetration Commission, 1940–1941, Durban, 1941.
35. See D.R. Bugwandeen's *A People on Trial for Breaking Racism: The Struggle for Land and Housing of the Indian People in Natal, 1940–1946*, Durban: Madiba Publishers, 1991.
36. The NIA committee members were: A.M.M. Lockhat, S. Rustomjee, P.R. Pather, J.W. Godfrey, A.S. Kajee. The NIC members were: A.I. Kajee, V. Lawrence, A.M. Moola, M.A.H. Moosa, V.K. Pillay, W.S. Seethal, and Hans Maghrajh. The Indian high commissioner gave the NIC *de facto* recognition, but the NIA was regarded as the official organisation by the government of India. NIC-NIA Deputation to Cape Town, 8 May 1943, Carter-Karis collection on microfilm.
37. NIC Agenda Book: Fifth Provincial Conference, 19–20 February 1944, Durban.
38. *Indian Views*, 14 August 1942.
39. Vishnu Padayachee, Shahid Vawda, and Paul Tichmann, *Indian Workers and Trade Unions in Durban, 1930–1950*, Durban: Institute for Social and Economic Research Report no.20, University of Durban-Westville, 1985.
40. *Indian Views*, 15 July 1935.
41. *South African Indian Who's Who and Commercial Directory*, Pietermaritzburg: Natal Witness, 1939; G.H. Calpin, *A.I. Kajee: His Work for the South African Indian Community*, Durban: Iqbal Study Group, n.d.; Conversation with I.C. Meer, 23 August 1993, Verulam. Pauline Podbrey's father approached Kajee to help him secure a licence for his shop. Kajee, who had some influence with

the white mayor 'picked up the receiver, snapped out an order . . . and the licence was granted'. Podbrey to author, 20 March 1995.

42. Pather's conversations with Tom Karis, 26 March 1964, Carter-Karis collection on microfilm.
43. Pather's links with important white individuals were well established by the 1960s, and he appeared to measure his own importance on the yardstick of his relationships with them. In a letter to Professor Gwendolen M. Carter, 2 April 1964, Pather wrote that he was sorry she could not attend his daughter's wedding, a 'brilliant', 'multi-racial' affair. Then he listed the names of white dignitaries who had attended. Carter-Karis collection on microfilm.
44. NIC Agenda Book: Third Provincial Conference and Annual General Meeting, 14 September 1941, Durban.
45. Even as early as 1932, the SAIC was considering passive resistance. In that year, it left groups in the Transvaal to use passive resistance if they desired, but did not openly endorse such action. The law in question was the Transvaal Asiatic Land Tenure Act of 1932. The agent-general of India, Sir Kunwar Maharaj Singh, who was present at the meeting, said to the passive resisters, 'I want to say that I cannot support you, and the Indian Government will not support you.' Minutes of the SAIC Annual Conference, 27 August 1932, Johannesburg.
46. NIC Agenda Book: Fifth Provincial Conference, 19–20 February 1944, Durban.
47. *Indian Opinion*, 28 April, 5 and 17 May, 7 July, 17 November, and 7 December 1944.
48. See SAIC Agenda Book: SAIC Annual Conference, Seventeenth Session, 8–10 February 1946, Johannesburg.
49. Ibid.
50. NIC Agenda Book: First Biennial Conference, 31 May – 1 June 1947.
51. Ibid. *Leader*, 25 August, 15 September, 20 and 27 October 1945; see also D.R. Bugwandeen's *A People on Trial*, pp.85–104, 108–14.
52. Edgar Brookes, for example, advised moderation in his speech at the 1950 NIC conference. See NIC Agenda Book: Fourth Annual Provincial Conference, 30 September – 2 October 1950, Durban.
53. Hugh Tinker, *Separate and Unequal: Indians in the British Commonwealth, 1920–1950*, Bombay: Vikas Publishing House, pp.219–39, 249–53.

*Notes*

## Chapter 4
## The New Leaders: 1945–1961

1. Padayachee et al., pp. vii, 10, 21, 33, 48; Bill Freund, *Insiders and Outsiders: The Indian Working Class of Durban, 1910–1990*, Portsmouth, London and Pietermaritzburg: Heinemann, James Currey and University of Natal Press, 1995.
2. Padayachee et al, pp. 50, 56–57.
3. Ibid., pp. 43, 89–122.
4. Ibid., pp. 154–56; Podbrey to author, 20 March 1995.
5. *Leader*, 17 March 1989.
6. Ibid., 10 August 1990. Conversation with Hassen E. Mall, 14 July 1993, Durban.
7. *Indian Opinion*, 14 July, 22 and 29 August 1941; 13 and 20 February 1942, 8 and 27 May 1942. Also conversation with I. C. Meer, 23 August 1993, Verulam.
8. *Leader*, 8 February 1988, 26 February and 5 March 1993.
9. Ibid., 31 March 1989.
10. *Indian Opinion*, 8 and 15 January 1943.
11. Ibid., 30 November 1935. P. R. Pather was one of the speakers.
12. Ibid., 15 November 1935. The intention to hold a bazaar was announced on 16 December 1935.
13. Ibid., 22 November 1935.
14. Naicker, 'What I owe to Mahatma Gandhi', 16 September 1948, Carter-Karis collection on microfilm.
15. Conversations with I. C. Meer, 23 August 1993, Verulam, and with Hassen E. Mall, 14 July 1993, Durban. The quotation is from the *Leader*, 10 August 1990.
16. Carter-Karis collection on microfilm; Thomas Karis and Gwendolen M. Carter (eds), *From Protest to Challenge: A Documentary History of African Politics in South Africa, 1882–1964*, 4 vols, Stanford, California: Hoover Institution Press, 1972–1977, vol. 4, p. 109; see also Edward Roux's *Time Longer Than Rope: A History of the Black Man's Struggle for Freedom in South Africa*, Madison: University of Wisconsin Press, 1965, p. 359; Pauline Podbrey, *White Girl in Search of the Party*, Pietermaritzburg: Hadeda Books, 1993, pp. 58–61, 71–75, 79, 90–91, 122–23, 157–201; Podbrey to author, 20 March 1995.
17. Karis and Carter, *From Protest to Challenge*, vol. 4, p. 109.
18. Ibid., p. 108.
19. Ibid., p. 143.
20. Carter-Karis collection on microfilm.
21. *Indian Who's Who*; Lawrence Papers, UNISA Documentation Centre for African Studies, Pretoria; Conversations with Sylvia Lawrence, 11 July 1993, Durban, and M. J. C. Naidoo, 21 August 1993, Durban.

22. Karis and Carter, *From Protest to Challenge*, vol.4, pp.86–87, 143. See also Jordan K. Ngubane, *An African Explains Apartheid*, Westport, Connecticut: Greenwood Press, 1976. Conversation with I.C. Meer, 23 August 1993, Verulam.

23. Conversation with Hassen E. Mall, 11 July 1993, Durban.

24. *Indian Views*, 20 and 27 May 1938. See also the autobiography of Dr Goonam who was a student at the same institution as Naicker: *Coolie Doctor: An Autobiography*, Durban: Madiba Publishers, 1991.

25. Karis and Carter, *From Protest to Challenge*, vol.4, pp.145–46.

26. Carter-Karis collection on microfilm.

27. Conversations with I.C. Meer, 23 August 1993, Verulam; H.E. Mall, 14 July 1993, Durban; and A.M. Kathrada, 31 August 1993, Johannesburg; *Guardian*, 20 October 1949; see also Alan Doyle's profile on Dadoo in *Guardian*, 15 December 1949.

28. Alan Doyle, Profile on Dadoo in *Guardian*, 15 December 1949; Karis and Carter, *From Protest to Challenge*, vol.4, pp.21–22; Ngubane, *An African Explains Apartheid*, pp.112–73; E.S. Reddy (ed.), *Dr Yusuf Mohamed Dadoo: His Speeches, Articles and Correspondence with Mahatma Gandhi, 1939–1983*, Durban: Madiba Publishers, 1991.

29. Carter-Karis collection on microfilm; Karis and Carter, *From Protest to Freedom*, vol.4, p.48–49; *Weekly Mail*, October 1989.

30. See Goonam's *Coolie Doctor*.

31. Carter-Karis collection on microfilm; *Leader*, 2 October 1946.

32. Philip Bonner, Peter Delius and Deborah Posel (eds), *Apartheid's Genesis, 1935–1962*, Johannesburg: Wits University Press, 1993, p.17.

33. Conversations with H.E. Mall, 14 July 1993, Durban, I.C. Meer, 23 August 1993, Verulam, and Ahmed Bhoola, 20 July 1993, Durban.

## Chapter 5
## Broadening the Front: 1940s and 1950s

1. NIC Agenda Book: First Biennial Conference, 31 May – 1 June 1947, Durban. The 9 November 1945 deputation consisted of: Monty Naicker, George Singh, M.D. Naidoo, M.R. Parekh, Hajee E.H. Ismail, I.M. Bawa, B. Goorden, B.A. Maharaj, and D.D. Lalla. The eleven-member PRC that met on 6 May 1946, consisted of: Monty Naicker, M.D. Naidoo, A.E. Patel, S.V. Reddy, H.A. Seedat, R.G. Pillay, M.P. Pillay, M.P. Naicker, P.B.A. Reddy, M. Moodliar, R.A. Pillay, and Debi Singh.

2. The 31 May – 1 June 1947 NIC Agenda Book listed the following PRC members for the Cape Province: Z. Gool, Sundra Pillay, Cassim Amra, and Yusuf Motala from Cape Town; M.M. Desai, V.K. Moodley, S.V. Appavoo from Port Elizabeth; and Dr N.V. Appavoo, Ms D. Jonathan, and R. Harry from East London.
3. The passive resisters were: Monty Naicker, M.D. Naidoo, Luxmi Govender, Veerama Pather, Ms Z. Asvat, Mrs Jamila Bhabha, Ms Zohra Bhayat, Mrs Amina Pahad, Mrs Patel, and Messrs J. Premlall, R.A. Pillay, V. Patrick, Shaik Mahomed, M.N. Govender, P. Poonsamy, V.S. Chetty, T.J. Vasie, and Abhai Soobramoney.
4. NIC Agenda Book: First Biennial Conference, 31 May – 1 June 1947, Durban.
5. Ibid; *Leader*, 31 August, 14, 21 and 28 September 1946. The 28 September 1946 issue has useful statistics.
6. *Indian Opinion*, 20 June 1947.
7. Ibid., 21 November 1947, 5 and 26 December 1947.
8. *Weekly News Bulletin*, 15 September 1947; *Weekly Overseas News Bulletin*, 31 August 1947, September 1947; *Flash*, 12 February 1948; TIC: Souvenir Programme – Farewell Reception to Our National Leaders, Johannesburg, 31 January 1947; *Passive Resister*, 2 October 1946, 29 November 1946, 6 December 1946, 17 January 1947, 21 February 1946, 7 March 1947, 16 May 1947, 23 May 1947, 30 May 1947, 26 June 1947, 10 July 1947, 24 July 1947, 6 August 1948, 14 August 1947, 28 August 1947, 20 November 1947, 6 February 1948, 10 July 1948, 16 July 1948.
9. NIC Agenda Book: Second Provincial Conference, 29–31 May 1948, Durban.
10. Ibid. See also *Victims of Racial Oppression*, a 36-page pamphlet prepared by H.A. Naidoo and Sorabjee Rustomjee, n.d. Tinker's *Separate and Unequal* deals with developments at UNO.
11. J.D. Rheinallt to Revd W.H. Satchell, 8 April 1947, Records of the SAIRR, Department of Historical Papers, University of the Witwatersrand; see memorandum submitted to UNO by the Council for Asiatic Rights, September 1947, Carter-Karis collection on microfilm.
12. NIC Agenda Book: Third Annual Conference, 24–26 June 1949, Durban; *Guardian*, 15 February 1951.
13. SAIO Agenda Book: First Conference, 20–22 April 1951, Johannesburg. The 26 November 1948 deputation consisted of: I.D. Coovadia, A.S. Kajee, M.N. Parekh, A.I. Minty, E.I. Haffejee, M.A.H. Moosa, G.H.A. Kathrada, Aboo Suliman, Habib V. Keshavjee, Revd B.L.E. Sigamoney, A. Bhabha, O.H. Mahomed, E. Nakhooda, M.M. Gardee, Cassim Hajee Osman.

*Notes*

14. *The Passive Resister*, 29 November 1946.
15. Minutes of Working Committee Meetings, 9 and 23 January, 13 February 1947, Records of the ANC, Department of Historical Papers, University of the Witwatersrand.
16. NIC Agenda Book: Third Annual Conference, 24–26 June 1949, Durban.
17. SAIC Agenda Book: Nineteenth Session, 15–17 September 1950, Johannesburg.
18. NIC Agenda Book: Fourth Annual Provincial Conference, 30 September – 2 October 1950, Durban.
19. The SAIC invited the following ANC officials: Dr J.S. Moroka (1950), Dr S.M. Molema (1952), and Chief A.J. Lutuli (1953, 1954, and 1955); the NIC invited the following ANC officials: Chief Lutuli (1951, 1953), Walter Sisulu (1954), Dr Arthur E. Latele (1956), and G.A. Mbeki (1957).
20. SAIC Agenda Book: Twentieth Session of the SAIC, 25–27 January 1952, Johannesburg. Dr Molema opened the conference.
21. Ibid.
22. SAIC Agenda Book: Nineteenth Session, 15–17 September 1950, Johannesburg; SAIC Agenda Book: Twentieth Session, 25–27 January 1952; see also NIC Agenda Book: Fifth Annual Conference, 29 September – 1 October 1951, Durban.
23. *Leader*, 15 and 19 September 1952; 'Ashwin Choudree Speaks', Records of the ANC, Department of Historical Papers, University of the Witwatersrand.
24. Report of the NIC Organisation, December 1952, and Memorandum by Monty Naicker, December 1952 [?], Treason Trials Records, Department of Historical Papers, University of the Witwatersrand; NIC Agenda Book: Sixth Annual Provincial Conference, 21–22 February 1953, Durban.
25. SAIC Agenda Book: Twenty-second Conference, 19–21 October 1956, Johannesburg; *Leader*, 10 September 1954; conversations with Billy Nair, 20 July 1995, and Hassen Mall 19 July 1995 in Durban. See also Ismail Vadi, *The Congress of the People and the Freedom Charter*, New Delhi: Sterling Publisher, 1995, pp. 87–96.
26. NIC Agenda Book: Twelfth Annual Provincial Conference, 9–11 October 1959, Durban.
27. NIC Agenda Book: Eighth Annual Provincial Conference, 25–27 March 1955, Durban.
28. Among those on trial for treason were: Monty Naicker, N.T. Naicker, I.C. Meer, Debi Singh, Gopallal Hurbans, Dr M.M. Motala, Billy Nair, M.P. Naicker, V.S.M. Pillay, K. Moonsamy, Thandray, Desai, Dr Padayachee.
29. See SAIC Agenda Book: Twenty-second Conference, 19–21 October 1956, Johannesburg.

30. NIC Agenda Book: Thirteenth Annual Provincial Conference, 3–5 March 1961, Pietermaritzburg.
31. Freund, *Insiders and Outsiders*.

## Chapter 6
## Routine Business: 1920s to 1961

1. NIC Agenda Book: Secretarial Report, 1 May 1938 for Activities of Congress from 1 January 1936 to 30 April 1938, Durban, 1938.
2. NIC Agenda Book: NIC Second Provincial Conference, 29–31 May 1948, Durban.
3. The branches listed for 1940 and 1941 were located in: Dannhauser, Dundee, Estcourt, Glencoe, Greytown, Howick, Isipingo, Ladysmith, Newcastle, Pietermaritzburg, Port Shepstone, Verulam, and Vryheid.
4. Minutes of Durban NIC Working Committee, 19 August 1956, and Minutes of Merebank NIC Working Committee, 31 July, 21 August, 11 September, 20 September, 2 October, and 18 December 1955, and 5 February, 4 March, 25 March, 29 April, and 22 July 1956, Records of Treason Trials, Department of Historical Papers, University of the Witwatersrand.
5. NIC Agenda Book: NIC Third Provincial Conference and Annual General Meeting, 14 September 1941, Durban; NIC Agenda Book: NIC First Biennial Conference, 31 May – 1 June 1947, Durban; NIC Agenda Book: NIC Fifth Annual Conference, 29 September – 1 October 1951, Durban. The major overseas contributors were Asians in East Africa.
6. NIC Agenda Book: NIC First Conference, 10–11 December 1938, Durban.
7. NIC Agenda Book: NIC Fourth Annual Conference, 30 September – 2 October 1950, Durban; NIC Agenda Book: NIC Sixth Annual Provincial Conference, 21–22 February 1953, Durban; NIC Agenda Book: NIC Seventh Annual Provincial Conference, 5–7 February 1954, Durban. The opponents were: A.I. Meer, A.I. Bhoola, A.C. Meer, and A.K.M. Docrat. Copies of the documents on the NIC assets are to be found in the S.S. Singh Collection, UNISA Documentation Centre for African Studies, Pretoria.
8. NIC Agenda Book: First Conference, 10–11 December 1938, Durban; NIC Agenda Book: Report of Activities, 1 May 1938 to 26 August 1938, Submitted to AGM of NIC, 27 August 1939, Durban.
9. This document provides a detailed account of Indian settlement in Natal around 1940. Final Statement submitted by the Natal

*Notes*

Indian Association to the Indian Penetration Commission, 1940–1941, Durban, 1941. See also: NIC Agenda Book: Third Provincial Conference and Annual General Meeting, 14 September 1941, Durban.

10. NIC Agenda Book: Fifth Provincial Conference, 19–20 February 1944, Durban; NIC Agenda Book: NIC First Biennial Conference, 31 May – 1 June 1947, Durban; NIC Agenda Book: First Biennial Conference, 31 May – 1 June 1947, Durban; NIC Agenda Book: Second Provincial Conference, 29–31 May, 1948, Durban.

11. NIC Agenda Book: Fourth Annual Provincial Conference, 30 September – 2 October 1950, Durban; NIC Agenda Book: Fifth Annual Conference, 29 September – 1 October 1951, Durban; NIC Agenda Book: Sixth Annual Provincial Conference, 21–22 February 1953, Durban.

12. NIC Agenda Book: Sixth Annual Conference, 21–23 February 1953, Durban.

13. NIC Agenda Book: Ninth Annual Conference, 22–24 June 1956, Durban.

14. NIC Agenda Book: Paper on Group Areas Act by Dr G.M. Naicker presented to the Conference on Group Areas Act convened by the NIC, 5–6 May 1956, Durban.

15. NIC Agenda Book: Eleventh Annual Provincial Conference, 21–23 November 1958, Durban.

16. NIC Agenda Book: Twelfth Annual Provincial Conference, 9–11 October 1959, Durban.

17. NIC Agenda Book: Thirteenth Annual Provincial Conference, 3–5 March 1961, Pietermaritzburg.

18. SAIC Agenda Book: SAIC Conference: Nineteenth Session, 15–17 September 1950, Johannesburg; SAIC Agenda Book: SAIC Conference: Twenty-first Session, July 1954, Durban; SAIC Agenda Book: SAIC Conference: Twenty-second Session, 19–21 October 1956, Johannesburg.

19. Memorandum by P.R. Pather, SAIO, Seventy Years of Frustration and Unhappiness: An Examination of Land and Trading Rights as they Affect Indians in Natal and Transvaal and a Ccriticism of the Group Areas Act of 1950, Durban.

20. SAIO Agenda Book: First Conference, 20–22 April 1951, Johannesburg.

21. Memorandum by Central Durban Property Protection Committee, 13, 14 November 1961, presented to the Group Areas Board. Carter-Karis collection.

22. NIC Agenda Book: Secretarial Report, 1 May 1938 for NIC activities from 1 January 1936 to 30 April 1938; NIC Agenda Book: First Conference, 10–11 December 1938, Durban.

23. See Final Statement submitted by the Natal Indian Association to

the Indian Penetration Commission, 1940–1941, Durban, 1941, Carter-Karis collection on microfilm.
24. NIC Agenda Book: Second Provincial Conference, 29–31 May 1948, Durban; NIC Testimony, Durban Native Administration Commission, Durban, 21 November 1947, Carter-Karis collection on microfilm; NIC Agenda Book: Fourth Annual Provincial Conference, 30 September – 2 October 1950, Durban.
25. NIC Agenda Book: Eighth Annual Provincial Conference, 25–27 March 1955, Durban.
26. NIC Agenda Book: Twelfth Annual Provincial Conference, 9–11 October 1959, Durban.
27. Agenda Books: Durban Combined Indian Ratepayers' Association Conference on Group Areas, Housing and Franchise, 25 October 1959, 23 July 1961, Durban; see also Memorandum by the Mayville Indian Ratepayers Association against zoning in Mayville, Cato Manor, Manor Gardens, Candilla, and Stella Hills for whites, 30 April 1958, Carter-Karis collection on microfilm.
28. NIC Agenda Book: Fourth Annual Provincial Conference, 30 September – 2 October 1950, Durban.
29. NIC Agenda Book: Eight Annual Conference, 25–27 March 1955, Durban; NIC Agenda Book: Ninth Annual Conference, 22–24 June 1956, Durban; NIC Agenda Book: Tenth Annual Conference, 22–24 November 1957, Durban; NIC Agenda Book: Thirteenth Annual Provincial Conference, 3–5 March 1961.
30. NIC Agenda Book: Tenth Annual Conference, 22–24 November 1957, Durban.
31. Ibid.
32. P.R. Pather, Indian Education Committee Conference, 15 October 1955; Indian Education Committee, Secretarial Report, April 1953 – October 1955 by P. Raidoo.
33. NIC Agenda Book: Third Annual Conference, 24–26 June 1949, Durban; NIC Agenda Book: Fourth Annual Conference, 30 September – 2 October 1950, Durban; NIC Agenda Book: Fifth Annual Conference, 29 September – 1 October 1951, Durban; NIC Agenda Book: Sixth Annual Conference, 21–22 February 1953, Durban; NIC Agenda Book: Seventh Annual Conference, 5–7 February 1954, Durban; NIC Agenda Book: Eighth Annual Conference, 25–27 March 1955, Durban; NIC Agenda Book: Ninth Annual Conference, 22–24 June 1956, Durban; NIC Agenda Book: Tenth Annual Conference, 22–24 November 1957, Durban; NIC Agenda Book: Eleventh Annual Conference, 21–23 November 1958, Durban; NIC Agenda Book: Twelfth Annual Conference, 9–11 October 1959, Durban; NIC Agenda Book: Thirteenth Annual Conference, 3–5 March 1961, Pietermaritzburg.

34. Ibid.
35. NIC Agenda Book: Third Annual Conference, 24–26 June 1949, Durban.
36. NIC Agenda Book: Second Provincial Conference, 29–31 May 1948, Durban; NIC Agenda Book: Thirteenth Annual Conference, 3–5 March 1961, Pietermaritzburg.
37. NIC Agenda Book: Third Annual Conference, 24–26 June 1949, Durban.
38. NIC Agenda Book: Secretarial Report: 1 May 1938 for activities of Congress from 1 January 1936 to 30 April 1938, Durban; NIC Agenda Book: First Conference, 10–11 December 1938, Durban; NIC Third Provincial Conference and AGM, 14 September 1941, Durban.
39. NIC Agenda Books from 1938 to 1944.
40. NIC Agenda Books from 1947 to 1961.
41. Those 'listed' as communists were: Cassim Amra, G. Ponnen, I.C. Meer, M.G. Naicker, M.P. Naicker, S.V. Reddy, D.A. Seedat, J.N. Singh and others.
42. NIC Agenda Book: Fourth Annual Provincial Conference, 30 September – 2 October 1950, Durban.
43. SAIO Agenda Book: First Conference, 20–22 April 1951, Johannesburg.
44. SAIC Agenda Book: Twenty-second Conference, 19–21 October 1956, Johannesburg.

## Chapter 7
### Revival and Resurgence: 1971–1990

1. Some works on the Black Consciousness Movement are: Robert Falton Jr., *Black Consciousness in South Africa: The Dialectics of Ideological Resistance to White Supremacy*, Albany, NY: State University of New York Press, 1986; Gail M. Gerhart, *Black Power in South Africa: The Evolution of an Ideology*, Berkeley: University of California Press, 1978; David Hirschman, 'The Black Consciousness Movement in South Africa', *Journal of Modern African Studies* 28: 1 (1990), pp. 1–22; Yunus Mohamed, 'The Power of Consciousness: Black Politics, 1967–77' in *Repression and Resistance: Insider Account of Apartheid*, pp.250–70, edited by Robin Cohen, Yvonne Muthien, and Abebe Zegeye, London: Hans Zell, 1990; Mokgethi Motlhabi, *The Theory and Practice of Black Resistance to Apartheid: A Social-Ethical Analysis*, Johannesburg: Skotaville, 1984, pp.106–53.
2. Statement by Mewalal Ramgobin, 1985. Karis-Gerhart collection. (This statement was part of the defence Ramgobin prepared for his 1985 treason trial.)

*Notes*

3. NIC Constitution as amended in 1972, Karis-Gerhart collection.
4. 'History of the Natal Indian Congress', 1985, 59 pages (unpublished manuscript prepared by Mewa Ramgobin), Karis-Gerhart collection.
5. NIC Annual Conference, Minutes, 20–22 July 1973, Kajee Memorial Hall, Durban. Karis-Gerhart collection. The two Pietermaritzburg members were: A.S. Chetty and R. Paparam.
6. The members of the subcommittee were: A.S. Chetty (convenor), Ela Ramgobin, R. Paparam, Mannie Jacobs, A.H. Randaree, D. Behari, Bala Mudaly, and M.J. Naidoo.
7. 'History of the Natal Indian Congress'.
8. SASO to all SRC's: A Memorandum Regarding the NIC's Charge, by N. Pityana, 3 March 1972, Karis-Gerhart collection.
9. NIC Annual Conference, 20–22 July 1973, Durban; NIC Presidential Address and Secretarial Report, 17–18 November 1978, Durban; NIC Presidential Address and Secretarial Report, 22–23 April 1977, Durban, Karis-Gerhart collection.
10. NIC Presidential Address and Secretarial Report, 17–18 November 1978, Durban.
11. NIC Annual Conference, 20–22 July 1973, Durban; NIC Annual Conference, 22–23 April 1977, Presidential Address and Secretarial Report, Durban; 'History of the Natal Indian Congress'.
12. Surendra Bhana and Bridglal Pachai (eds), *A Documentary History of Indian South Africans*, Cape Town: David Philip, 1984, p.276.
13. *Survey of Race Relations in South Africa, 1981*, Johannesburg: South African Institute of Race Relations, 1982, pp.17–21.
14. Bhana and Pachai, p.285.
15. Ibid., p.279. See also pp.256–60, 260–64, 269–70.
16. Huntington delivered a keynote address at the Biennial Political Science Association of South Africa Conference, Rand Afrikaans University, 17 September 1981, which was published as, 'Reform and Stability in a Modernizing, Multi-Ethnic Society', *Politikon: South African Journal of Political Science* 8: 2 (December 1981), pp.8–26.
17. NIC Annual Conference, 17–18 November 1978, Durban, Karis-Gerhart collection.
18. The NIC's Stand on the Constitutional Proposals, 12 pp., 1982 or 1983, Karis-Gerhart collection.
19. NIC's Position on the New Constitutional Proposals, 33 pp., 1983, Karis-Gerhart collection.
20. A statement by a commission that had investigated the feasibility of a united front was issued on 23 January 1983. I do not know more about the commission. See Julie Frederikse, *The Unbreak-*

*able Thread: Non-racialism in South Africa*, Bloomington: Indiana University Press, 1990, pp.178–80; Mark Swilling, 'The United Democratic Front and Township Revolt', in *Popular Struggles in South Africa*, pp.90–113, edited by William Cobbett and Robin Cohen, Trenton, NJ: Africa World Press, 1988.

21. The transcripts of the NIC meetings were used in the prosecution of sixteen UDF defendants who were charged with high treason in 1985. Leading NIC individuals such as Mewa Ramgobin, George Sewpershad, and M.J. Naidoo were involved. They were accused of using the UDF as a front for the banned ANC. Karis-Gerhart collection.

22. The speakers at the four meetings were: Phoenix: Paul David, A. Moodley, Zac Yacoob, Ela Ramgobin, Solly Limbada, Richard Gumede, George Sewpershad, Archie Gumede, Mrs Naicker, R.D. Naidu, Thumba Pillay, and I.M. Singh; Marburg: S.R. Joseph, M.J. Naidoo, Rabbi Bugwandeen, Fatima Meer, Billy Nair, Mewa Ramgobin, R.B. Chaudary, and Peter Govender; Ladysmith: Iqbal Khan, Dr A.H. Sader, Fatima Meer, Ebrahim Bawa, Mewa Ramgobin, Patrick 'Terror' Lekota, and Dr Allan Boesak; Newcastle: Aroon Bhoogal, George Sewpershad, Manibhen Sita, Fatima Meer, Dr E.E. Jassat, Billy Nair, and Mewa Ramgobin. The transcripts of these meetings are part of the Karis-Gerhart collection.

23. In the Transvaal, an Anti-Constitutional Proposal Committee (ACPC) had been founded in May 1978 by Dr R.A.M. Salojee's Lenasia People's Candidate Party and by Dr I. Variava's Lenasia Action Committee. The ACPC was replaced a year later by the Solidarity Front. The Transvaal Anti-SAIC Committee (TASC) was created to fight the SAIC elections in 1981. TASC was broadened in 1983 to fight the new constitution. See *Survey of Race Relations in South Africa, 1983*, Johannesburg, 1984, pp.36–43.

24. See fn.22.

25. Ibid.

26. Ibid.

27. One joke related a hypothetical situation in which Raj and Botha went to a restaurant and inquired of the Indian waiter, 'Do you serve crabs?', to which the waiter replied, 'We serve anybody.' In another hypothetical situation, Raj and Botha visited the Valley of a Thousand Hills where they played the echo-game. When Raj shouted 'Rubbish,' no echo came back. On Botha's advice, Raj tried again but this time he shouted, 'I want to be a prime minster.' Back came the echo: 'Rubbish, rubbish, rubbish.'

28. See Martin Murray, *South Africa, Time of Agony, Time of Des-*

*tiny: The Upsurge of Popular Protest*, London: Verso, 1987, pp. 250–51. The six were UDF's president Archie Gumede, and NIC's George Sewpersadh, Mewa Ramgobin, Billy Nair, M.J. Naidoo, and Paul David. M.J. Naidoo related to the author that the group had considered other options such as, for example, demonstrating in front of Parliament, but members feared being detected and detained before getting to Cape Town. The group decided to occupy the consulate after making sure that it enjoyed the same diplomatic immunity as an embassy. Conversation with M.J. Naidoo, 14 July 1995, Durban.

29. Some of the works I have referred to are: Jeremy Baskin, *Striking Back: A History of Cosatu*, Johannesburg: Ravan, 1991; Stephen Ellis and Tsepo Sechaba, *Comrades Against Apartheid: The ANC and the South African Communist Party in Exile*, Bloomington: Indiana University Press, 1992, pp. 141–74; Jonathan Hyslop, 'School Student Movements and State Education Policy, 1922–87', in *Popular Struggles in South Africa*, pp. 183–209; Steven Mufson, *Fighting Years: Black Resistance and the Popular Struggle for a New South Africa*, Boston: Beacon Press, 1990, pp. 13–272; Murray, *Time of Agony*, pp. 129–430; Robert M. Price, *The Apartheid State in Crisis: Political Transformation in South Africa, 1975–1990*, New York: Oxford University Press, 1991, pp. 152–219; Hilary Sapire, 'Politics and Protest in Shack Settlements of the Pretoria-Witwatersrand-Vereeniging Region, South Africa, 1980–1990', *Journal of Southern African Studies*, 18: 3 (September 1992), pp. 670–92; Jeremy Seekings, '"Trailing Behind the Masses": The United Democratic Front and Township Politics in the Pretoria-Witwatersrand-Vaal Region, 1983–84', *Journal of Southern African Studies* 18: 1 (March 1991), pp. 93–114; and Ari Sitas, 'The Making of the "Comrades" Movement in Natal, 1985–91', *Journal of Southern African Studies* 18: 3 (September 1992), pp. 629–41.

30. Mufson, *Fighting Years*, pp. 321–23; Heather Hughes, 'Violence in Inanda, August 1985', *Journal of Southern African Studies* 13: 3 (April 1987), pp. 331–54; and Kumi Naidoo, 'The Politics of Youth Resistance in the 1980s: The Dilemmas of a Differentiated Durban', *Journal of Southern African Studies* 18: 1 (March 1991), pp. 143–65.

31. Mufson, *Fighting Years*, pp. 269–71. On the cabal issue see also 'Report and Recommendations of Commission on the "Cabal", late 1980', 12 pp., and 'Robben Islanders take a frank and critical look at the political situation in Natal, the way forward', early 1990s, 8 pp. Both copies were supplied by Dr Iain Edwards of the Killie Campbell Africana Library, University of Natal, Durban.

32. Murray, *Time of Agony*, pp. 431–39; Stephen M. Davis, *Apartheid's Rebels: Inside South Africa's Hidden War*, New Haven: Yale University Press, 1987, p. 115.
33. Price, *Apartheid State*, p. 225, 226–29.
34. Ibid., p. 269.
35. Ibid., see chart on p. 240.
36. *Weekly Mail*, 8–11 March 1991.

**Chapter 8**
**Conclusion**

1. Gary D. Klein, 'Sojourning and Ethnic Solidarity: Indian South Africans', *Ethnic Groups* 8 (1990), pp. 1–13.
2. *Indian Opinion*, 11 January 1918, 10 February 1952.
3. *Indian Opinion*, 4 February 1916, 16 March 1917.
4. Conversation with I. C. Meer, 23 August 1993, Verulam.
5. Yunus Carrim, 'The Natal Indian Congress: Decision on a New Thrust Forward', *Work in Progress* 52 (1988), pp. 39–46.
6. Price, *Apartheid State*.
7. R. Singh and S. Vawda, 'What's in a Name?: Some Reflections on the Natal Indian Congress', *Transformations* 6 (1988), pp. 1–21.
8. Carrim, 'Natal Indian Congress', pp. 39, 43.
9. Conversation with Ela Gandhi, 19 July 1993, Professor Vishnu Padayachee, 7 July 1995, Shahid Vawda, 11 July 1995, M.J. Naidoo, 14 July 1995, Hassim Seedat 17 July 1995, and Billy Nair, 20 July 1995, all in Durban. See also 'Report and Recommendations of Commission on the "Cabal", late 1980', 12 pp., and 'Robben Islanders take a frank and critical look at the political situation in Natal, the way forward', early 1990s, 8 pp. Both copies were supplied by Dr Iain Edwards of the Killie Campbell Africana Library, University of Natal, Durban.
10. *New Nation*, 17–18 June 1992.
11. *Weekly Mail*, 26 March – 7 April 1993.
12. Conversation with Ibrahim I. Ibrahim, 19 August 1993, Johannesburg.

# BIBLIOGRAPHY

**Primary Sources**
Biographies of Political Activists, Documentation Centre, University
   of Durban-Westville, Durban.
Harry G. Lawrence Papers, J.W. Jagger Library, University of Cape
   Town, Cape Town.
Vincent Lawrence Papers, Documentation Centre for African Studies,
   University of South Africa, Pretoria.
Ponnen, George, 'Life and Times of George Ponnen', unpublished
   manuscript, Documentation Centre, University of Durban-
   Westville, Durban, 240 pp.
Records of the ANC, Department of Historical Papers, University of
   the Witwatersrand, Johannesburg.
E.S. Reddy Collection, United Nations and South Africa, 1946–1962,
   Documentation Centre, University of Durban-Westville, Durban.
J.D. Rheinallt Jones Papers, Records of the South African Institute of
   Race Relations, Department of Historical Papers, University of
   the Witwatersrand, Johannesburg.
S.S. Singh Collection, Documentation Centre for African
   Studies, University of South Africa, Pretoria.
Treason Trials Records, Department of Historical Papers, University
   of the Witwatersrand, Johannesburg.


*Natal Indian Congress*
NIC Agenda Book: Secretarial Report, 1 May 1938, for Activities of
   Congress from 1 January 1936 to 30 April 1938, Durban, 1938.
NIC Agenda Book: First Conference, 10–11 December 1938, Durban.
NIC Agenda Book: Report on Activities from 1 May 1938 to 26 August
   1939, Durban.
NIC Agenda Book: General Meeting, 9 June 1940, Durban.
NIC Agenda Book: Third Provincial Conference and Annual General
   Meeting, 14 September 1941, Durban.
NIC Agenda Book: General Meeting, 14 September 1941, Durban.
NIC Agenda Book: Fifth Provincial Conference, 19–20 February
   1944, Durban.
NIC Agenda Book: First Biennial Conference, 31 May – 1 June 1947,
   Durban.
NIC Testimony to Durban Native Administration Commission, 21
   November 1947.
NIC Agenda Book: Second Annual Provincial Conference, 29–31 May
   1948, Durban.

# Bibliography

NIC Agenda Book: Third Annual Provincial Conference, 24–26 June 1949, Durban.

NIC Agenda Book: Fourth Annual Provincial Conference, 30 September – 2 October 1950, Durban.

NIC Agenda Book: Fifth Annual Provincial Conference, 29 September – 1 October 1951.

NIC Agenda Book: Sixth Annual Provincial Conference, 21–22 February 1953.

NIC Agenda Book: Seventh Annual Provincial Conference, 5–7 February 1954, Durban.

NIC Agenda Book: Eighth Annual Provincial Conference, 25–27 March 1955, Durban.

NIC Group Areas Conference: Paper on the Group Areas Act by G.M. Naicker, 5–6 May 1956, Durban.

NIC Agenda Book: Ninth Annual Provincial Conference, 22–24 June 1956, Durban.

NIC Agenda Book: Tenth Annual Provincial Conference, 22–24 November 1957, Durban.

NIC Agenda Book: Eleventh Annual Provincial Conference, 21–23 November 1958, Durban.

NIC Agenda Book: Twelfth Annual Provincial Conference, 9–11 October 1959, Durban.

NIC Agenda Book: Thirteenth Annual Provincial Conference, 3–5 March 1961, Pietermaritzburg.

NIC Constitution as amended, 1972

NIC Annual Conference, Minutes, 20–22 July 1973, Durban.

NIC Presidential Address and Secretarial Report, 20–22 September 1974, Durban.

NIC Presidential Address and Secretarial Report, 26 March 1976, Durban.

NIC Presidential Address and Secretarial Report, 22–23 April 1977, Durban.

NIC Presidential Address and Secretarial Report, 17–18 November 1978, Durban.

NIC's Stand on the Constitutional Proposals, 1982 or 1983, 12 pp.

NIC's Position on the New Constitutional Proposals, 1983, 33 pp.

NIC Anti-election Meeting: Marburg, Port Shepstone, 22 July 1984, transcript made by the security police, and used in the Pietermaritzburg treason trial, 1985.

NIC Anti-election Meeting: Ladysmith, 1 August 1984, transcript made by the security police, and used in the Pietermaritzburg treason trial, 1985.

NIC Anti-election Meeting: Phoenix, Durban, 11 December 1983, transcript made by the security police, and used in the Pietermaritzburg treason trial, 1985.

## Bibliography

NIC Anti-election Meeting: Newcastle, 18 August 1984, transcript made by the security police and used in the Pietermaritzburg treason trial, 1985.

'History of the Natal Indian Congress', unpublished manuscript prepared by Mewa Ramgobin, 1985, 59 pp.

*South African Indian Congress*

SAIC Agenda Book: Emergency Conference of the South African Indian Congress, 5–6 October 1930.

SAIC Annual Conference, 27 August 1932, Johannesburg.

SAIC Agenda Book: Annual Conference, Fifteenth Session, 17–18 February 1935, Durban.

SAIC Memoranda submitted to government ministers, 1935–1939.

SAIC Agenda Book: Annual Conference, Sixteenth Session, 26–28 June 1943, Johannesburg.

SAIC Agenda Book: Annual Conference, Seventeenth Session, 8–10 February 1946, Johannesburg.

SAIC Agenda Book: Annual Conference, Nineteenth Session, 15–17 September 1950, Johannesburg.

SAIC Agenda Book: Annual Conference, Twentieth Session, 25–27 January 1952, Johannesburg.

SAIC Agenda Book: Annual Conference, Twenty-first Session, July 1954, Durban.

SAIC Presidential Address by G.M. Naicker at Annual Conference, Twenty-second Session, 1955.

SAIC Agenda Book: Annual Conference, Twenty-second Session, 19–21 October 1956, Johannesburg.

*South African Indian Organisation*

SAIC Agenda Book: SAIO Inaugural Conference, 11–12 September 1948, Durban.

SAIO Agenda Book: First Conference, 20–22 April 1951, Johannesburg.

*Transvaal Indian Congress*

TIC Agenda Book: Provincial Conference, Johannesburg, 26 June 1938.

TIC Memorandum to the Transvaal Asiatic Land Laws Commission, n.d., 45 pp.

TIC: Souvenir Programme, Farewell Reception to Our National Leaders, Johannesburg, 31 January 1947.

TIC: Fourteenth Annual Conference, 26 April 1959, Johannesburg.

# Bibliography

*Miscellaneous*

Non-European United Front: Conference, Statements, Minutes of the First Non-European Conference, 23–25 June 1927, Kimberley.

Non-European United Front: Conferences, Statements, Minutes of the Second Non-European Conference, January 1930, Cape Town.

Non-European United Front: Minutes of the Third Non-European Conference, 5–8 January 1931, Bloemfontein.

CBSIA Agenda Book: First Natal Provincial Conference of the Colonial-Born and Settler Indian Association, 31 December 1933 – 2 January 1934, Durban.

Non-European United Front of South Africa, Conference, 8–10 April 1939, Cape Town.

Final Statement submitted by the Natal Indian Association to the Indian Penetration Commission, 1940–1941, Durban, 1941.

Non-European Unity Movement: Minutes of the Fourth Unity Conference, 19–20 December 1945, Kimberley.

Non-European Unity Conference, 1–5 January 1945, Cape Town.

Non-European Unity Movement: Proceedings of the Fifth Unity Conference, 20–21 December 1946, Kimberley.

Memorandum by Council for Asiatic Rights to United Nations Organisation, September 1947.

Non-European Unity Movement: Proceedings of the Sixth Unity Conference, 28–30 March 1948, Cape Town.

'What I owe to Mahatma Gandhi', by G. M. Naicker, Durban, September 16, 1948, 5 pp.

Secretarial Report by P. Raidoo, Indian Education Committee, April 1953 – October 1955.

ANC-SAIC Memorandum to United Nations Organisation on Racial Discrimination in South Africa, 28 July 1954, 10 pp.

Address by P. R. Pather, Indian Education Committee Conference, 15 October 1955, Durban.

Ideological Trends in Indian Congress, 1956, 6 pp.

Memorandum by Mayville Indian Ratepayers' Association against zoning in Mayville, Cato Manor, Manor Gardens, Candilla, and Stella Hills for Whites, 30 April 1958, Durban.

Agenda Books: Durban Combined Indian Ratepayers' Association Conference on Group Areas, Housing, and Franchise, 25 October 1959, 23 July 1961, Durban.

Memorandum by Central Durban Property Protection Committee, 13,14 November 1961, presented to the Group Areas Board by A. M. Moola and P. R. Pather, Durban.

Statements by Nana Sita at his trial under Group Areas Act, magistrate's court, Pretoria, 7 August 1967, 18 pp.

# 173

## Bibliography

Statement prepared by M.J. Naidoo for his defence in the Pieter-maritzburg treason trial, 1985.
Statement prepared by Mewalal Ramgobin for his defence in the Pietermaritzburg treason trial, 1985.
Report and Recommendations of the Commission on the 'Cabal', late 1980s, 12 pp.
Robben Islanders Take a Frank and Critical Look at the Political Situation in Natal, the Way Forward, early 1990s, 8 pp.

*Interviews*
Ahmed I. Bhoola, 20 July 1993, Durban
Ela Gandhi, 19 July 1993, Durban
Pravin Gordhan, 25 August 1993, Durban
Ibrahim I. Ibrahim, 9 August 1993, Johannesburg
Ahmed Kathrada, 31 August 1993, Johannesburg
Sylvia Lawrence, 11 July 1993, Durban
Hassen E. Mall, 14 July 1993, 19 July 1995, Durban
Ismail C. Meer, 23 August 1993, Verulam
M.J. Naidoo, 14 July 1995, Durban
M.J.C. Naidoo, 21 August 1993, Durban
Billy Nair, 25 August 1993, 20 July 1995, Durban
Vishnu Padayachee, 7 July 1995, Durban
Mewa Ramgobin, 23 August 1993, Durban
Cassim Saloojee, 28 July 1993, Johannesburg
Hassim Seedat, 17 July, 19 August 1993, 17 July 1995, Durban
Shahid Vawda, 11 July 1995, Durban

*Newspapers*
*Advance*, 1952–54
*The Call*, February to July 1940
*Guardian*, 1949–52
*Graphic*, 1952–58, 1973
*Indian Opinion*, 1907–61
*Indian Views*, 1935–48
*Leader*, 1945–46, 1952–55, 1960–61, 1971–72, 1978, 1988–93
*New Age*, 1955–59, 1961–62
*Passive Resister*, July 1946 – October 1948

**Secondary Sources**
Aiyar, P.S., *Conflict of Races in South Africa: Long-range Segregation Programme*, Durban, 1946.

## Bibliography

Babenia, Natoo, *Memoirs of a Saboteur: Reflections on My Political Activity in India and South Africa, as told to Iain Edwards*, Bellville: Mayibuye Books, 1995.

Baskin, Jeremy, *Striking Back: A History of Cosatu*, Johannesburg: Ravan, 1991.

Beall, J.D. and D. North-Coombes, 'The 1913 Disturbances in Natal: The Social and Economic Background to "Passive Resistance"', *Journal of Natal and Zulu History* 6 (1983) pp.48–81.

Bhana, Surendra (ed), *Essays on Indentured Indians in Natal*, Leeds, Yorkshire: Peepal Tree Press, 1990.

_____, *Indentured Indian Emigrants to Natal, 1860–1902: A Study Based on Ships' Lists*, New Delhi: Promilla & Co., 1991.

Bhana, Surendra and U.S. Dhupelia, 'Passive Resistance Among Indian South Africans: A Historiographical Survey', *South African Historical Journal* 16 (November 1984) pp.118–31.

Bhana, Surendra and B. Pachai (eds), *A Documentary History of Indian South Africans, 1860–1982*, Cape Town: David Philip, 1984.

Bhana, Surendra and J.B. Brain, *Setting Down Roots: Indian Migrants in South Africa, 1860–1911*, Johannesburg: Wits University Press, 1990.

Bonner, Philip, Peter Delius, and Deborah Posel (eds), *Apartheid's Genesis, 1935–1962*, Johannesburg: Ravan Press, Wits University Press, 1993.

Brown, Judith and Martin Prozesky (eds), *Gandhi and South Africa: Principles and Politics*, Pietermaritzburg and New York: University of Natal Press and St. Martin's Press, 1996.

Bugwandeen, D.R., *The Struggle for Land and Housing of the Indian People of Natal, 1940–1946*, Durban: Madiba, 1991.

Carrim, Yunus, 'The Natal Indian Congress: Decision on a New Thrust', *Work in Progress* 52 (1988), pp.39–46.

Dadoo, Y.M., *Statement by Y.M. Dadoo, 6 September 1940, at his Trial in Johannesburg*, Johannesburg: Non-European United Front, 1940.

_____, *The Indian People in South Africa. Facts about the Ghetto Act*, Johannesburg: Communist Party, 1946.

Davis, Stephen M., *Apartheid's Rebels: Inside South Africa's Hidden War*, New Haven: Yale University Press, 1987.

Ellis, Stephen and Tsepo Sechaba, *Comrades Against Apartheid: The ANC and the South African Communist Party in Exile*, Bloomington: Indiana University Press, 1992.

Fatton, Robert Jr., *Black Consciousness in South Africa: The Dialectics of Ideological Resistance to White Supremacy*, Albany, NY: State University of New York Press, 1986.

175

## Bibliography

*Five Months of Struggle: A Brief Account of the Passive Resistance Campaign from 13 June to 13 November 1946*, Durban n.d..

Frederikse, Julie, *The Unbreakable Thread: Nonracialism in South Africa*, Bloomington: Indiana University Press, 1990.

Freund, Bill, '"It is my work": Labour Segementation, Militancy and the Indian Working Class of Durban,' Centre for African Studies Seminar Paper, University of Cape Town, 6 May 1992.

_____, 'The Destruction of Communities, 1930–1980: The Indian Working Class of Durban and the Group Areas Act', African Studies Institute Seminar Paper, University of the Witwatersrand, 30 August 1993.

_____, *Insiders and Outsiders: The Indian Working Class of Durban, 1910–1990*, Portsmouth, London, Pietermaritzburg: Heinemann, James Currey, University of Natal Press, 1995.

Gandhi, M.K., *Satyagraha in South Africa*, Ahmedabad: Navajivan, 1928.

_____, *The Story of My Experiments with Truth*, Washington: Public Affairs Press, 1948.

_____, *The Collected Works of Mahatma Gandhi*, vols 1 to 12, New Delhi: Government Printer, 1958–.

Gerhart, Gail M., *Black Power in South Africa: The Evolution of an Ideology*, Berkeley: University of California Press, 1978.

Ginwala, Frene, 'Class, Consciousness, and Control – Indian South Africans, 1860–1914', (Ph.D. thesis, Oxford University, 1974).

Goonam, K., *Coolie Doctor: An Autobiography*, Durban: Madiba, 1991.

Guest, Bill and John M. Sellers (eds), *Enterprise and Exploitation in a Victorian Colony: Aspects of the Economic and Social History of Colonial Natal*, Pietermaritzburg: University of Natal Press, 1985.

*Golden Number of Indian Opinion: Souvenir of Passive Resistance Movement in South Africa, 1906–1914*, Pietermaritzburg, 1914.

Hirschman, David, 'The Black Consciousness Movement in South Africa', *Journal of Modern African Studies* 28:1 (1990) pp.1–22.

*History of Indian Immigration into South Africa*, n.p., 1946[?].

Hughes, Heather, 'Violence in Inanda, August 1985', *Journal of Southern African Studies* 13:3 (April 1987) pp.331–354.

Hunt, James D., *Gandhi in London*, New Delhi: Promilla, 1978.

Huttenback, R.A., *Gandhi in South Africa: British Imperialism and the Indian Question, 1860–1914*, Ithaca, New York: Cornell University Press, 1971.

Johnson, Robert E., 'Indians and Apartheid in South Africa: The Failure of Resistance', (Ph.D. thesis, University of Massachusetts, 1973).

Joshi, P.S., *The Tyranny of Colour: A Study of the Indian Problem in South Africa*, 1942.

## Bibliography

Kajee, A.I., P.R. Pather, and A. Christopher, *Treatment of Indians in South Africa: A Memorandum of Facts*, Cape Town: SAIC, 1946.

Karis, Thomas and G. Carter (eds), *From Protest to Challenge: A Documentary History of African Politics in South Africa, 1882–1964*, vols 1 to 4, Stanford: Hoover Institution Press, 1972–1977.

Klein, Gary D., 'Sojourning and Ethnic Solidarity: Indian South Africans', *Ethnic Groups* 8 (1990), pp. 1–13.

Kuper, Hilda, *Indian People in Natal*, Pietermaritzburg: University of Natal Press, 1960.

Kuper, Leo, *Passive Resistance in South Africa*, New Haven: Yale University Press, 1957.

Lodge, Tom, *Black Politics in South Africa Since 1945*, London: Longman, 1983.

_____, 'Paper Monuments: Political Biography in the New South Africa', *South African Historical Journal* 28 (1993), pp. 249–63.

Lodge, Tom et al., *All Here and Now: Black Politics in South Africa in the 1980s*, Ford Foundation, 1991.

Mahadevan, T.K., *The Year of the Phoenix: Not a Novel*, New Delhi, 1982.

Meer, Fatima (ed), *Treason Trial*, Durban: Madiba, 1989.

_____ (ed), *The South African Gandhi: An Abstract of the Speeches and Writings of M.K. Gandhi, 1893–1914*, Durban: Madiba, 1996.

Mesthrie, U.S., 'From Sastri to Desmukh: A Study of the Role of the Government of India's Representative in South Africa, 1927 to 1946', (Ph.D. thesis, University of Natal, 1987).

_____, 'Indian National Honour versus Trader Ideology: Three Unsuccessful Attempts at Passive Resistance in the Transvaal, 1932, 1939, and 1941', *South African Historical Journal* 21 (1989), pp. 39–54.

Mohamed, Yunus, 'The Power of Consciousness: Black Politics, 1967–77' in *Repression and Resistance: Insider Account of Apartheid*, edited by Robin Cohen, Yvonne Muthien, and Abebe Zegeye, London: Zell Publishers, 1990, pp. 250–70.

Mufson, Steven, *Fighting Years: Black Resistance and the Popular Struggle for a New South Africa*, Boston: Beacon Press, 1990.

Murray, Martin, *South Africa, Time of Agony, Time of Destiny: The Upsurge of Popular Protest*, London: Verso, 1987.

Naidoo, Jay, 'Clio and the Mahatma', *Journal of Southern African Studies* 16:4 (December 1990), pp. 741–50.

Naidoo, Kumi, 'The Politics of Youth Resistance in the 1980s: The Dilemmas of a Differentiated Durban', *Journal of Southern African Studies* 18:1 (March 1991), pp. 143–65.

Naidoo, M.D., *Round Table Conference: Our Views*, Durban, 1947[?].

Ngubane, Jordan K., *An African Explains Apartheid*, Westport, Connecticut: Greenwood Press, 1976.
*Ninety Fighting Years, 1894–1984: The Natal Indian Congress – A Pictorial History for a United, Free and Democratic South Africa*, Durban, 1984.
Omi, Michael and Winant, Howard, *Racial Formation in the United States from the 1960s to the 1980s*, New York: Routledge, 1986.
Pachai, B., *International Aspect of the South African Indian Question, 1860–1971*, Cape Town: Struik, 1971.
_____ (ed.) *South Africa's Indians: The Evolution of a Minority*, Washington, D.C.: University Press of America, 1979.
Padayachee, Vishnu, Shahid Vawda, and Paul Tichmann, *Indian Workers and Trade Unions in Durban, 1930–1950*, Durban: Institute for Social and Economic Research Report no. 20, University of Durban-Westville, 1985.
Padayachee, Vishnu and Robert Morrell, 'Indian Merchants, and Dukawallahs in the Natal Economy, c. 1875–1914', *Journal of Southern African Studies* 17:1 (March 1991), pp. 71–102.
Pahad, Essop, 'The Development of Indian Political Movements in South Africa, 1924–1946', (Ph.D. thesis, University of Sussex, 1972).
Palmer, Mabel, *History of Indians in Natal*, Cape Town: Oxford University Press, 1957.
Pather, P. R., *Seventy Years of Frustration and Unhappiness: An Examination of Land and Trading Rights as they Affect Indians in Natal and Transvaal and a Criticism of the Group Areas Act of 1950*, SAIO, 1950.
Podbrey, Pauline, *White Girl in Search of the Party*, Pietermaritzburg: Hadeda Books, 1993.
Power, Paul F., 'Gandhi in South Africa', *Journal of Modern African Studies* 7:3 (1969), pp. 441–55.
Price, Robert M., *The Apartheid State in Crisis: Political Transformation in South Africa, 1975–1990*, New York: Oxford University Press, 1991.
Ramgobin, Mewa, 'Action Towards a Non-violent Society: The Relevance of Gandhi to South Africa', *Africa Quarterly* 28:3–4 (1988–89), pp. 52–59.
Reddy, E. S.(ed.), *Monty Speaks: The Speeches of Dr G. M. Naicker, 1945–1963*, Durban: Madiba, 1991.
_____ (ed.), *Yusuf Mohamed Dadoo: His Speeches, Articles and Correspondence with Mahatma Gandhi, 1939–1983*, Durban: Madiba, 1991.
_____, *Gandiji: Vision of a Free South Africa*, New Delhi: Sanchar Publishing House, 1995.

# Bibliography

Reddy, E.S. and G. Gandhi (eds), *Gandhi and South Africa, 1914–1918*, Ahmedabad: Navajivan, 1993.

Reddy, E.S. and Fatima Meer (eds), *Passive Resistance, 1946: A Selection of Documents*, Durban: Madiba, 1996.

Roux, Edward, *Time Longer Than Rope: A History of the Black Man's Struggle for Freedom in South Africa*, Madison: Wisconsin University Press, 1965.

Singh, R. and S. Vawda, 'What's in a Name?: Some Reflections on the Natal Indian Congress', *Transformations* 6 (1988), pp. 1–21.

Sitas, Ari, 'The Making of the "Comrades" Movement in Natal, 1985–91', *Journal of Southern African Studies* 18:3 (September 1992), pp. 629–41.

*South Africa Defies United Nations: What Next?* Passive Resistance Council of South Africa, October 1947.

*South African Political Materials: A Catalogue of the Carter-Karis Collection*, Bloomington, Indiana: Southern African Research Archives Project, 1977.

Stone, J.H. II, 'M.K. Gandhi: Some Experiments with Truth', *Journal of Southern African Studies* 16:4 (December 1990), pp. 721–740.

Swilling, Mark, 'The United Democratic Front and Township Revolt' in *Popular Struggles in South Africa*, edited by William Cobbett and Robin Cohen, Trenton, New Jersey: Africa World Press, 1988, pp. 90–113.

Swan, M.J. *Gandhi: The South African Experience*, Johannesburg: Ravan Press, 1985.

_____, 'Ideology in Organised Indian Politics, 1891–1948' in *The Politics of Race, Class, and Nationalism in Twentieth Century South Africa*, edited by S. Marks and S. Trapido, New York: Longman, 1987, pp. 182–206.

Tinker, Hugh, *Separate and Unequal: India and the Indians in the British Commonwealth, 1920–1950*, Delhi: Vikas Publishing House, 1976.

Vadi, Ismael, *The Congress of the People and the Freedom Charter Campaign*, New Delhi: Sterling, 1995.

Vahed, Goolam H., 'The Making of Indian Identity in Durban, 1914–1949', (Ph.D. thesis, Indiana University, 1995).

*Victims of Racial Oppression*, Durban: South African Passive Resistance Council, 1946[?].

White, W.B., 'Passive Resistance in South Africa, 1946–48', *Journal of Natal and Zulu History* 5 (1982), pp. 1–28.

*Index*

# Index

185

*Index*

Pachy, S.P.  117
Paddison deputation  35
Palmer, Mabel  74
Pan Africanist Congress (PAC)
    119, 133
Pandit, Vijaylakshmi  75
Paruk, E.M.  33, 45, 47, 50, 96,
    142
Pass laws  82
Passive Resistance Council  72,
    73, 74, 79
*Passive Resister*  63, 75
Patel, Ahmed E.  69
Patel, B.M.  143
Pather, P.R.  39, 47, 48–9, 52,
    53, 98, 104, 143
Pather, V.S.C.  33, 142
Patidar Association  27, 141
Pegging Act *see* Occupation of
    Land (Transvaal and Natal)
    Restriction Act of 1943
Percy, N.K.  69
Peters, Billy  56, 69
Phoenix Settlement  17, 117,
    131
Pillai, V.S.M.  69
Pillay, A.D.  11
Pillay, Krishensamy  78
Pillay, R.A.  73
Polak, H.S.L.  20, 30
Ponnen, George  41, 56, 69
Population Registration Act  82
President's Council  124–5, 129
Pretoria Agreement  51–2, 101
Price, Robert M.  145
Public Safety Act  84
Pundit, Ram Sunder  26

Rajbansi, Amichand  129
Ramesar, Paul  117
Ramesar, R.  117, 119
Ramgobin, Mewa  117, 120, 126,
    128, 147
Rana, C.N.  98

Randeria, H.J.  98
Randeria, S.G.  142
Randeria, S.J.  25
Reagan, Ronald  130, 132
Reciprocity Act of 1944  54
Reddy, Bill  117
Reddy, S.V.  94
*Resist the Ghetto Act*  75
Rheinallt Jones, J.D.  78
Riots (1949)  81, 111
Rivonia trial  68
Rural Dealers' Ordinance of 1923
    111
Rustomjee, Parsee  25, 30
Rustomjee, Sorabjee  73, 143

Sader, *Dr* A.H.  99
Salisbury Island College  109
    *see also* University of
    Durban-Westville
Sam China Tournament  139
Sammy, Ponoo Veloo  37
Sanatan Ved Dharma Sabha
    26, 137
SAR and H Indian Employees'
    Union  142
Saraswathee Samarsa
    Sungeetha Drama Company
    138
Sastri College  108
Sastri, V.S.S.  42
Satyagraha  25
Satyagraha campaign  14, 16,
    22–31
Satyagrahis  23, 26
Schreiner, W.P.  22
Scott, *Revd* Michael  74
Searle decision  24
*Sechaba*  61
Seebran, Pasaw  98
Seedat, D.A.  41, 42, 56, 62
Separate Voters Representation
    Act  82
Sewpersadh, George  117, 120,
    149

*Index*

## Index